Praise for Jonathan Ba Research and Program

"I am often asked when there will be a proven prescription for weight loss. This is that prescription."
   - **Harvard Medical School's** Dr. Theodoros Kelesidis

"A treasure trove of reliable information...hot, hot hot!"
   - **Harvard Medical School's** Dr. JoAnne Manson

"Reveals the real story of diet, exercise, and their effects on us. I heartily recommend this." - **Harvard Medical School's** Dr. John J. Ratey

"Opens the black box of fat loss and makes it simple!"
   - **Dr. Oz's Personal Trainer** Joel Harper

"I'm a big fan" – **World's Top Trainer and Creator of P90X** Tony Horton

"Will do more to assist people with their health than all the diet books out there put together. I want to shout, 'Bravo! Finally someone gets it!'"
   - Dr. Christiane Northrup, **New York Times best-selling author** of *Women's Bodies, Women's Wisdom* and *The Wisdom of Menopause*

"Provides a powerful set of tools for creating lifelong health!"
   - Dr. Mark Hyman, **New York Times best-selling author** of *The Blood Sugar Solution* and *The Daniel Plan*

"An easily understood and applied framework that will change the way you live, look, and feel... will end your confusion once and for all."
   - Dr. William Davis, **New York Times best-selling author** of *Wheat Belly*

"Cuts through the noise around weight loss and tells it to us straight."
   - Dr. Sara Gottfried, **New York Times best-selling author** of *The Hormone Cure* and *The Hormone Reset Diet*

"Readers will find that focusing on the kinds of foods they are eating can boost their brain power and help them lose the extra ten pounds."
   - Dr. Daniel G. Amen, **New York Times best-selling author** of *Change Your Brain, Change Your Body*

"Will change the way you look at dieting!"
   - JJ Virgn, **New York Times best-selling author** of *The Virgin Diet*

See hundreds more medical reviews and success stories at:
www.SANESolution.com

To my best friend, partner, and wife, Angela. Just the thought of you brings me more joy, more satisfaction, and more life than anything else I have ever experienced. You are my beloved, without reservation or qualification, as we dance into eternity.

To my heroes and parents, Mary Rose and Robert. All that I am is thanks to your love, example, and support. From the day I was born, and every day after, you have always found a way to help and love me. I live, hoping to return the favor.

To my friends and partners, Scott, Tyler, Sean, Abhishek, April, Lori, Wednesday, Josh, Jason, Andrea, and Rebecca, my delightful sister Patty, my wonderful brothers Tim, Cameron, and Branden, and my loving in-laws Terry and Carolyn. You are such treasures. Thank you for being who you are and thank you for meaning so much to me.

To you and the hundreds of thousands of other SANE family members all around the world with the courage to eat and exercise smarter. You have taken the road less traveled and it will make all the difference.

Published in the Worldwide by Yopti, LLC (SANESolution) New York. Seattle. California. www.SANESolution.com.

SANE books can be purchased at quantity discounts to use as premiums, promotions, or for corporate training programs. For more information on bulk pricing please email Yopti, LLC at SANESolution.com/contact.

Editor: Mary Rose Bailor
Production: Abhishek Pandey
Exterior Design: Tyler Archer

Publisher's Cataloging-in-Publication
Bailor, Jonathan.
99 Calorie Myth & SANE Certified Green Smoothies (Updated and Expanded): The Most Hormonally Healing, Low-Sugar, Belly-Fat-Burning, and Energy Boosting Green Smoothie Recipes Ever Created! / Jonathan Bailor.—2nd ed.
p. cm.
1. Health   2. Weight Loss   3. Cooking   4. Recipes   5. Diet   6. Nutrition   7. Beverages
I. Bailor, Jonathan   II. Title.

Manufactured in the United States of America. First Edition.

The information expressed here is intended for educational purposes only. This information is provided with the understanding that neither Jonathan Bailor nor Yopti, LLC nor SANESolution nor affiliates are rendering medical advice of any kind. This information is not intended to supersede or replace medical advice, nor to diagnose, prescribe or treat any disease, condition, illness or injury. It is critical before beginning any eating or exercise program, including those described in this and related works, that readers receive full medical clearance from a licensed physician.

TABLE OF CONTENTS

TIP: Not familiar with the SANE Food Group or SANE Serving Sizes?

It's all good! Get everything you need by attending your FREE masterclass at SANESeminar.com and by downloading your FREE tools at SANESolution.com/Tools.

Get Everything You Need To Burn Fat and Prepare Delicious Meals at the SANE Store

Fat-Burning Flour

Mood-Boosting Chocolate Powder

Clean Pea Protein

Craving Killer Bake-N-Crisps

Slimming Sugar Substitute

Clean Whey Protein

Vanilla Almond Meal Bars

Craving Killer Chocolate Truffle

 No Added Sugar

 100% Natural

 Gluten Free

 No GMO's

 No Dairy

 No Soy

SANE™

Find all of these EXCLUSIVE tools, plus over 100 other fat-burning SANE products to help you and your family look and feel your best!

Visit Today: Store.SANESolution.com

PREFACE

Welcome to the SANE family! Jonathan Bailor here and I want to thank you again for taking time out of your hectic schedule to ensure that your dinner table is for savoring and smiles, not self-criticism and calorie math. Eating should be a source of joy and wellness, not shame and sickness. I sincerely hope that our time together will open your eyes to how easy it can be to reach your weight and fitness goals once you break free from the confusing and conflicting outdated theories and lies that have trapped you for so long.

If you only take one thing away from this book let it be this: Any weight problem you may be experiencing is not your fault! I know that may sound trite, but it's true. How can you be expected to lose those annoying pounds when all you've been given is outdated science and methods from the 1960's that have been proven NOT to work.

My mission is to not only reshape your body, but it's also to reshape the way you think about weight loss. What that means is I will be here with you every step of the way to provide all the support and tools you need to finally reach your weight loss goals. Whether you need to lose a few extra pounds around your belly, are looking for a complete body transformation, want all-day energy, or just want to make sense of all the confusing and conflicting health information out there once and for all, you are finally in the right place!

TIP: Be sure to add service@SANESolution.com to your email safe senders list/address book. This ensures you get all your upcoming SANE bonus recipes, tools, and how-to videos.

So if you are ready to stop counting calories... Ready to stop killing yourself with exercise you hate... Ready to end your struggle with weight... and are tired of being hungry and tired...this is your chance. It's time to get off the dieting roller-coaster once and for all. **Are you ready?**

I urge you to make a commitment to yourself to continue this journey. You are worth it. After all, you took action to get this book so that means you are ready and willing to step up and make positive changes. If you follow the simple and scientifically backed principles we teach, **I promise you will lose weight...and keep it off for good.**

You are part of the family now, and I am so excited to have you here as we bust the myths that have been holding you back... perhaps for years. Remember this...**now is your time**, and these are your proven tools for lasting weight loss success. Welcome home.

Can't wait to meet you at
SANESolution.com,

Jonathan Bailor
New York Times Bestselling Author,
SANE Founder, and soon...your
personal weight-loss coach

P.S. Over the years I have found that our most successful members, the ones who have lost 60, 70, even 100 pounds...and kept it off...are the ones who started their personal weight-loss plan on our FREE half-day Masterclass. It's your best opportunity to fall in love with the SANE lifestyle, learn exactly how to start making the simple changes that lead to dramatic body transformations, and get introduced to your new SANE family. **Be sure to reserve your spot now at http://SANESeminar.com.**

GET STARTED WITH SANE CERTIFIED GREEN SMOOTHIES

Your SANECertified™ green smoothies are radically different from the sugar saturated "healthy" smoothies you will find on grocery store shelves and served to you at smoothie chains. While those smoothies can contain **as much sugar as three cans of Coke**, your SANECertified™ green smoothies contain about as much sugar as a cup of fresh blueberries. They also contain no artificial sweeteners, unnatural chemicals or flavorings, are 100% gluten free, never contain any GMO ingredients, and are 100% kid-approved and family friendly. In short, your SANECertified™ green smoothies are the single most effective and safest beverage you and your family could ever enjoy. Simply by adding two to four of these smoothies to your family's daily routine, within one week you can:

- Lose weight
- Reverse aging
- Control diabetes
- End overeating
- Boost your ability to concentrate
- Improve heart health
- Lower risk of heart disease
- Enhance athletic performance
- Develop lean muscle
- Reduce risk of Alzheimer's disease
- Boost Mood

- Reduce hunger
- Reduce risk of cancer
- Curb cravings
- Get sick less often
- Sleep better and feel more rested
- Reduce anxiety
- Improve cholesterol and blood pressure
- Enhance bone density
- Boost fertility
- Reduce signs of acne and eczema
- Reduce chronic pain

- Clear away cellulite
- Increase energy
- Boost confidence
- Improve complexion
- Enhance strength and fitness
- Improve libido
- Increase insulin sensitivity
- Improve hormone levels
- Increase regularity
- Enjoy relief from IBS and migraines
- Speed-up metabolism

TIP: Not familiar with the SANE Food Group or SANE Serving Sizes?

It's all good! Get everything you need by attending your FREE masterclass at SANESeminar.com and by downloading your FREE tools at SANESolution.com/Tools.

THE TOP TWO WAYS TO USE SANE SMOOTHIES TO REACH YOUR GOALS

#1 - THE "ALL VEGGIE" SMOOTHIE

Goal: Easily increase your veggie intake.

Since the goal of these smoothies is **only** to increase your veggie intake, be sure to **exclude** any protein and healthy fats in the smoothie's ingredients list. These "all veggie" smoothies are the perfect way to add veggies to a meal which already contains protein and fat.

For example, drink one of these smoothies along with an egg (healthy fat) and egg white (protein) scramble to ensure your breakfast is a Complete SANE Meal (veggies, protein, and fat).

Also, these "all veggie" smoothies can be enjoyed throughout the day to help you easily reach your daily SANE Plan veggie servings goal.

#2 - THE "COMPLETE SANE MEAL" SMOOTHIE

Goal: Quickly prepare a convenient meal.

Since these smoothies serve as your entire meal, they should contain 2-5 servings of Non-Starchy Veggies, 1-2 servings of Nutrient-Dense Protein, and (if needed) 1-2 servings of Whole-Food Fats.

The most delicious and effective way to add Whole-Food Fats to any smoothie is to add a serving of unsweetened shredded coconut or avocado and then to blend as usual.

SANECertified Green Smoothie Recipes

BLACKBERRY BLAST

1 Serving   Prep: 1 min   Blend: 2 min   Total: 3 min
4 Non-Starchy Vegetables   1 Nutrient-Dense Protein   1 Low-Fructose Fruit

- 1 Cup Blackberries (frozen or fresh)
- 6 Cups Spinach
- 1 Medium Lemon (peeled)
- 1/2 TSP Cinnamon
- 2 TBSP Garden in My Glass*
- 4 TBSP Clean Whey Protein**
- 1 TSP Hormone Healing Green Tea (optional)
- 2 TBSP Slimming Sugar Substitute (optional)***

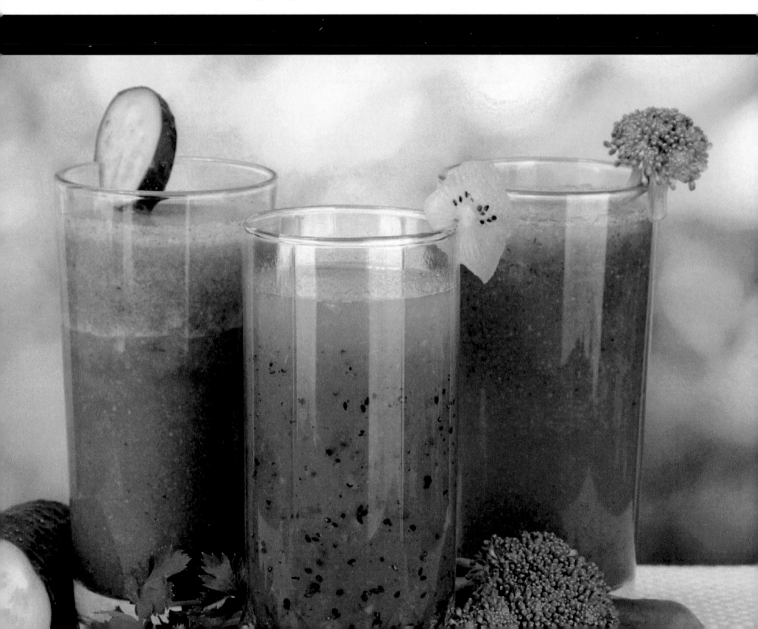

DIRECTIONS

- Add all ingredients to a high-powered blender with 8 oz. cold water and a handful of ice.

- Blend for 2 minutes or until completely blended (i.e. no pieces of veggies or fruit are visible).

- Adjust the amount of water and ice for desired consistency and desired temperature.

TIP: Can't find some of these ingredients at your local grocery store? Have them delivered quickly and easily by visiting your SANE Superfoods Store at http://store.SANESolution.com.

NOTES

*You can add two additional serving of Non-Starchy Vegetables in place of the two tablespoons of Garden in My Glass. If you do not add more veggies and you do not add Garden in My Glass, track only two servings of Non-Starchy Vegetables per smoothie (instead of four servings).

**Only add protein if the smoothie is your entire meal. Vegetarians can use 6 TBSP of Clean Pea Protein (instead of Clean Whey Protein).

***To minimize sugar content, reduce fruit (other than lemon) and increase Slimming Sugar Substitute. If fruit is reduced by half or more, no Low-Fructose Fruit servings should be tracked. Due to their extremely low sugar content, lemons should not be reduced and do not need to be tracked.

BLACKBERRY ESCAPE

1 Serving   Prep: 1 min   Blend: 2 min   Total: 3 min
4 Non-Starchy Vegetables   1 Nutrient-Dense Protein   1 Low-Fructose Fruit

- 1 Cup Blackberries (frozen or fresh)
- 2 Cups Chard
- 4 Cups Spinach
- 1 Medium Lemon (peeled)
- 1/2 TSP Cinnamon
- 2 TBSP Garden in My Glass*
- 4 TBSP Clean Whey Protein**
- 1 TSP Hormone Healing Green Tea (optional)
- 2 TBSP Slimming Sugar Substitute (optional)***

DIRECTIONS

- Add all ingredients to a high-powered blender with 8 oz. cold water and a handful of ice.

- Blend for 2 minutes or until completely blended (i.e. no pieces of veggies or fruit are visible).

- Adjust the amount of water and ice for desired consistency and desired temperature.

TIP: Can't find some of these ingredients at your local grocery store? Have them delivered quickly and easily by visiting your SANE Superfoods Store at http://store.SANESolution.com.

NOTES

*You can add two additional serving of Non-Starchy Vegetables in place of the two tablespoons of Garden in My Glass. If you do not add more veggies and you do not add Garden in My Glass, track only two servings of Non-Starchy Vegetables per smoothie (instead of four servings).

**Only add protein if the smoothie is your entire meal. Vegetarians can use 6 TBSP of Clean Pea Protein (instead of Clean Whey Protein).

***To minimize sugar content, reduce fruit (other than lemon) and increase Slimming Sugar Substitute. If fruit is reduced by half or more, no Low-Fructose Fruit servings should be tracked. Due to their extremely low sugar content, lemons should not be reduced and do not need to be tracked.

BLACKBERRY GLEE

1 Serving   Prep: 1 min   Blend: 2 min   Total: 3 min

4 Non-Starchy Vegetables   1 Nutrient-Dense Protein   1 Low-Fructose Fruit

- 1 Cup Blackberries (frozen or fresh)
- 2 Cups Chard
- 4 Cups Romaine Lettuce
- 1 Medium Lemon (peeled)
- 1/2 TSP Cinnamon
- 2 TBSP Garden in My Glass*
- 4 TBSP Clean Whey Protein**
- 1 TSP Hormone Healing Green Tea (optional)
- 2 TBSP Slimming Sugar Substitute (optional)***

DIRECTIONS

- Add all ingredients to a high-powered blender with 8 oz. cold water and a handful of ice.

- Blend for 2 minutes or until completely blended (i.e. no pieces of veggies or fruit are visible).

- Adjust the amount of water and ice for desired consistency and desired temperature.

TIP: Can't find some of these ingredients at your local grocery store? Have them delivered quickly and easily by visiting your SANE Superfoods Store at http://store.SANESolution.com.

NOTES

*You can add two additional serving of Non-Starchy Vegetables in place of the two tablespoons of Garden in My Glass. If you do not add more veggies and you do not add Garden in My Glass, track only two servings of Non-Starchy Vegetables per smoothie (instead of four servings).

**Only add protein if the smoothie is your entire meal. Vegetarians can use 6 TBSP of Clean Pea Protein (instead of Clean Whey Protein).

***To minimize sugar content, reduce fruit (other than lemon) and increase Slimming Sugar Substitute. If fruit is reduced by half or more, no Low-Fructose Fruit servings should be tracked. Due to their extremely low sugar content, lemons should not be reduced and do not need to be tracked.

BLUEBERRY BLISS

1 Serving   Prep: 1 min   Blend: 2 min   Total: 3 min

4 Non-Starchy Vegetables   1 Nutrient-Dense Protein   1 Low-Fructose Fruit

- 3/4 Cup Blueberries (frozen or fresh)
- 2 Cups Arugula
- 4 Cups Romaine Lettuce
- 1 Medium Lemon (peeled)
- 1/2 TSP Cinnamon
- 2 TBSP Garden in My Glass*
- 4 TBSP Clean Whey Protein**
- 1 TSP Hormone Healing Green Tea (optional)
- 2 TBSP Slimming Sugar Substitute (optional)***

DIRECTIONS

- Add all ingredients to a high-powered blender with 8 oz. cold water and a handful of ice.

- Blend for 2 minutes or until completely blended (i.e. no pieces of veggies or fruit are visible).

- Adjust the amount of water and ice for desired consistency and desired temperature.

TIP: Can't find some of these ingredients at your local grocery store? Have them delivered quickly and easily by visiting your SANE Superfoods Store at http://store.SANESolution.com.

NOTES

*You can add two additional serving of Non-Starchy Vegetables in place of the two tablespoons of Garden in My Glass. If you do not add more veggies and you do not add Garden in My Glass, track only two servings of Non-Starchy Vegetables per smoothie (instead of four servings).

**Only add protein if the smoothie is your entire meal. Vegetarians can use 6 TBSP of Clean Pea Protein (instead of Clean Whey Protein).

***To minimize sugar content, reduce fruit (other than lemon) and increase Slimming Sugar Substitute. If fruit is reduced by half or more, no Low-Fructose Fruit servings should be tracked. Due to their extremely low sugar content, lemons should not be reduced and do not need to be tracked.

BLUEBERRY DELIGHT

1 Serving   Prep: 1 min   Blend: 2 min   Total: 3 min
4 Non-Starchy Vegetables   1 Nutrient-Dense Protein   1 Low-Fructose Fruit

- 3/4 Cup Blueberries (frozen or fresh)
- 2 Cups Kale
- 4 Cups Spinach
- 1 Medium Lemon (peeled)
- 1/2 TSP Cinnamon
- 2 TBSP Garden in My Glass*
- 4 TBSP Clean Whey Protein**
- 1 TSP Hormone Healing Green Tea (optional)
- 2 TBSP Slimming Sugar Substitute (optional)***

DIRECTIONS

- Add all ingredients to a high-powered blender with 8 oz. cold water and a handful of ice.

- Blend for 2 minutes or until completely blended (i.e. no pieces of veggies or fruit are visible).

- Adjust the amount of water and ice for desired consistency and desired temperature.

TIP: Can't find some of these ingredients at your local grocery store? Have them delivered quickly and easily by visiting your SANE Superfoods Store at http://store.SANESolution.com.

NOTES

*You can add two additional serving of Non-Starchy Vegetables in place of the two tablespoons of Garden in My Glass. If you do not add more veggies and you do not add Garden in My Glass, track only two servings of Non-Starchy Vegetables per smoothie (instead of four servings).

**Only add protein if the smoothie is your entire meal. Vegetarians can use 6 TBSP of Clean Pea Protein (instead of Clean Whey Protein).

***To minimize sugar content, reduce fruit (other than lemon) and increase Slimming Sugar Substitute. If fruit is reduced by half or more, no Low-Fructose Fruit servings should be tracked. Due to their extremely low sugar content, lemons should not be reduced and do not need to be tracked.

BLUEBERRY RASPBERRY BLISS

1 Serving   Prep: 1 min   Blend: 2 min   Total: 3 min
4 Non-Starchy Vegetables   1 Nutrient-Dense Protein   1 Low-Fructose Fruit

- 1/3 Cup Blueberries (frozen or fresh)
- 3/4 Cup Raspberries (frozen or fresh)
- 2 Cups Arugula
- 4 Cups Romaine Lettuce
- 1 Medium Lemon (peeled)
- 1/2 TSP Cinnamon
- 2 TBSP Garden in My Glass*
- 4 TBSP Clean Whey Protein**
- 1 TSP Hormone Healing Green Tea (optional)
- 2 TBSP Slimming Sugar Substitute (optional)***

DIRECTIONS

- Add all ingredients to a high-powered blender with 8 oz. cold water and a handful of ice.

- Blend for 2 minutes or until completely blended (i.e. no pieces of veggies or fruit are visible).

- Adjust the amount of water and ice for desired consistency and desired temperature.

TIP: Can't find some of these ingredients at your local grocery store? Have them delivered quickly and easily by visiting your SANE Superfoods Store at http://store.SANESolution.com.

NOTES

*You can add two additional serving of Non-Starchy Vegetables in place of the two tablespoons of Garden in My Glass. If you do not add more veggies and you do not add Garden in My Glass, track only two servings of Non-Starchy Vegetables per smoothie (instead of four servings).

**Only add protein if the smoothie is your entire meal. Vegetarians can use 6 TBSP of Clean Pea Protein (instead of Clean Whey Protein).

***To minimize sugar content, reduce fruit (other than lemon) and increase Slimming Sugar Substitute. If fruit is reduced by half or more, no Low-Fructose Fruit servings should be tracked. Due to their extremely low sugar content, lemons should not be reduced and do not need to be tracked.

BLUEBERRY RASPBERRY BREEZE

1 Serving   Prep: 1 min   Blend: 2 min   Total: 3 min
4 Non-Starchy Vegetables   1 Nutrient-Dense Protein   1 Low-Fructose Fruit

- 1/3 Cup Blueberries (frozen or fresh)
- 3/4 Cup Raspberries (frozen or fresh)
- 2 Cups Kale
- 4 Cups Romaine Lettuce
- 1 Medium Lemon (peeled)
- 1/2 TSP Cinnamon
- 2 TBSP Garden in My Glass*
- 4 TBSP Clean Whey Protein**
- 1 TSP Hormone Healing Green Tea (optional)
- 2 TBSP Slimming Sugar Substitute (optional)***

DIRECTIONS

- Add all ingredients to a high-powered blender with 8 oz. cold water and a handful of ice.

- Blend for 2 minutes or until completely blended (i.e. no pieces of veggies or fruit are visible).

- Adjust the amount of water and ice for desired consistency and desired temperature.

TIP: Can't find some of these ingredients at your local grocery store? Have them delivered quickly and easily by visiting your SANE Superfoods Store at http://store.SANESolution.com.

NOTES

*You can add two additional serving of Non-Starchy Vegetables in place of the two tablespoons of Garden in My Glass. If you do not add more veggies and you do not add Garden in My Glass, track only two servings of Non-Starchy Vegetables per smoothie (instead of four servings).

**Only add protein if the smoothie is your entire meal. Vegetarians can use 6 TBSP of Clean Pea Protein (instead of Clean Whey Protein).

***To minimize sugar content, reduce fruit (other than lemon) and increase Slimming Sugar Substitute. If fruit is reduced by half or more, no Low-Fructose Fruit servings should be tracked. Due to their extremely low sugar content, lemons should not be reduced and do not need to be tracked.

BLUEBERRY RASPBERRY DELIGHT

1 Serving   Prep: 1 min   Blend: 2 min   Total: 3 min
4 Non-Starchy Vegetables   1 Nutrient-Dense Protein   1 Low-Fructose Fruit

- 1/3 Cup Blueberries (frozen or fresh)
- 3/4 Cup Raspberries (frozen or fresh)
- 2 Cups Kale
- 4 Cups Spinach
- 1 Medium Lemon (peeled)
- 1/2 TSP Cinnamon
- 2 TBSP Garden in My Glass*
- 4 TBSP Clean Whey Protein**
- 1 TSP Hormone Healing Green Tea (optional)
- 2 TBSP Slimming Sugar Substitute (optional)***

DIRECTIONS

- Add all ingredients to a high-powered blender with 8 oz. cold water and a handful of ice.

- Blend for 2 minutes or until completely blended (i.e. no pieces of veggies or fruit are visible).

- Adjust the amount of water and ice for desired consistency and desired temperature.

TIP: Can't find some of these ingredients at your local grocery store? Have them delivered quickly and easily by visiting your SANE Superfoods Store at http://store.SANESolution.com.

NOTES

*You can add two additional serving of Non-Starchy Vegetables in place of the two tablespoons of Garden in My Glass. If you do not add more veggies and you do not add Garden in My Glass, track only two servings of Non-Starchy Vegetables per smoothie (instead of four servings).

**Only add protein if the smoothie is your entire meal. Vegetarians can use 6 TBSP of Clean Pea Protein (instead of Clean Whey Protein).

***To minimize sugar content, reduce fruit (other than lemon) and increase Slimming Sugar Substitute. If fruit is reduced by half or more, no Low-Fructose Fruit servings should be tracked. Due to their extremely low sugar content, lemons should not be reduced and do not need to be tracked.

BLUEBERRY RASPBERRY MAGIC

1 Serving   Prep: 1 min   Blend: 2 min   Total: 3 min
4 Non-Starchy Vegetables   1 Nutrient-Dense Protein   1 Low-Fructose Fruit

- 1/3 Cup Blueberries (frozen or fresh)
- 3/4 Cup Raspberries (frozen or fresh)
- 2 Cups Arugula
- 4 Cups Spinach
- 1 Medium Lemon (peeled)
- 1/2 TSP Cinnamon
- 2 TBSP Garden in My Glass*
- 4 TBSP Clean Whey Protein**
- 1 TSP Hormone Healing Green Tea (optional)
- 2 TBSP Slimming Sugar Substitute (optional)***

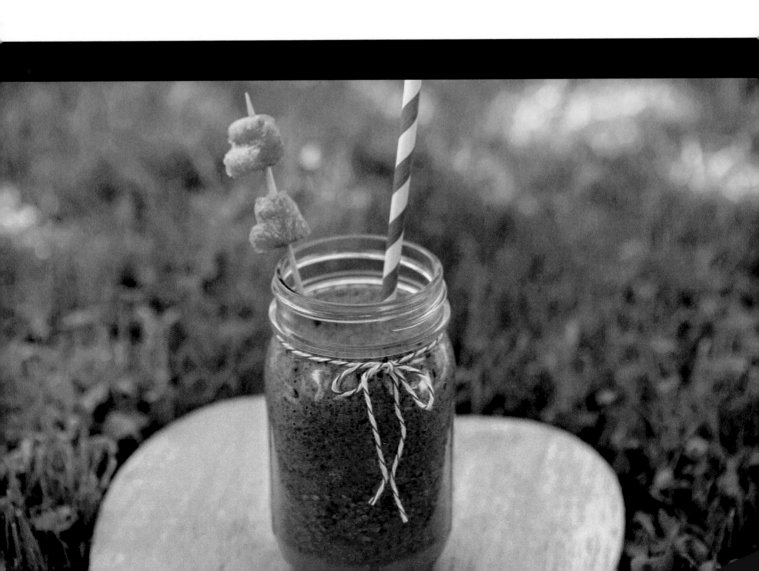

DIRECTIONS

- Add all ingredients to a high-powered blender with 8 oz. cold water and a handful of ice.

- Blend for 2 minutes or until completely blended (i.e. no pieces of veggies or fruit are visible).

- Adjust the amount of water and ice for desired consistency and desired temperature.

TIP: Can't find some of these ingredients at your local grocery store? Have them delivered quickly and easily by visiting your SANE Superfoods Store at http://store.SANESolution.com.

NOTES

*You can add two additional serving of Non-Starchy Vegetables in place of the two tablespoons of Garden in My Glass. If you do not add more veggies and you do not add Garden in My Glass, track only two servings of Non-Starchy Vegetables per smoothie (instead of four servings).

**Only add protein if the smoothie is your entire meal. Vegetarians can use 6 TBSP of Clean Pea Protein (instead of Clean Whey Protein).

***To minimize sugar content, reduce fruit (other than lemon) and increase Slimming Sugar Substitute. If fruit is reduced by half or more, no Low-Fructose Fruit servings should be tracked. Due to their extremely low sugar content, lemons should not be reduced and do not need to be tracked.

BLUEBERRY RASPBERRY SUNRISE

1 Serving   Prep: 1 min   Blend: 2 min   Total: 3 min
4 Non-Starchy Vegetables   1 Nutrient-Dense Protein   1 Low-Fructose Fruit

- 1/3 Cup Blueberries (frozen or fresh)
- 3/4 Cup Raspberries (frozen or fresh)
- 6 Cups Romaine Lettuce
- 1 Medium Lemon (peeled)
- 1/2 TSP Cinnamon
- 2 TBSP Garden in My Glass*
- 4 TBSP Clean Whey Protein**
- 1 TSP Hormone Healing Green Tea (optional)
- 2 TBSP Slimming Sugar Substitute (optional)***

DIRECTIONS

- Add all ingredients to a high-powered blender with 8 oz. cold water and a handful of ice.

- Blend for 2 minutes or until completely blended (i.e. no pieces of veggies or fruit are visible).

- Adjust the amount of water and ice for desired consistency and desired temperature.

TIP: Can't find some of these ingredients at your local grocery store? Have them delivered quickly and easily by visiting your SANE Superfoods Store at http://store.SANESolution.com.

NOTES

*You can add two additional serving of Non-Starchy Vegetables in place of the two tablespoons of Garden in My Glass. If you do not add more veggies and you do not add Garden in My Glass, track only two servings of Non-Starchy Vegetables per smoothie (instead of four servings).

**Only add protein if the smoothie is your entire meal. Vegetarians can use 6 TBSP of Clean Pea Protein (instead of Clean Whey Protein).

***To minimize sugar content, reduce fruit (other than lemon) and increase Slimming Sugar Substitute. If fruit is reduced by half or more, no Low-Fructose Fruit servings should be tracked. Due to their extremely low sugar content, lemons should not be reduced and do not need to be tracked.

BLUEBERRY SUNRISE

1 Serving   Prep: 1 min   Blend: 2 min   Total: 3 min
4 Non-Starchy Vegetables   1 Nutrient-Dense Protein   1 Low-Fructose Fruit

- 3/4 Cup Blueberries (frozen or fresh)
- 6 Cups Romaine Lettuce
- 1 Medium Lemon (peeled)
- 1/2 TSP Cinnamon
- 2 TBSP Garden in My Glass*
- 4 TBSP Clean Whey Protein**
- 1 TSP Hormone Healing Green Tea (optional)
- 2 TBSP Slimming Sugar Substitute (optional)***

DIRECTIONS

- Add all ingredients to a high-powered blender with 8 oz. cold water and a handful of ice.

- Blend for 2 minutes or until completely blended (i.e. no pieces of veggies or fruit are visible).

- Adjust the amount of water and ice for desired consistency and desired temperature.

TIP: Can't find some of these ingredients at your local grocery store? Have them delivered quickly and easily by visiting your SANE Superfoods Store at http://store.SANESolution.com.

NOTES

*You can add two additional serving of Non-Starchy Vegetables in place of the two tablespoons of Garden in My Glass. If you do not add more veggies and you do not add Garden in My Glass, track only two servings of Non-Starchy Vegetables per smoothie (instead of four servings).

**Only add protein if the smoothie is your entire meal. Vegetarians can use 6 TBSP of Clean Pea Protein (instead of Clean Whey Protein).

***To minimize sugar content, reduce fruit (other than lemon) and increase Slimming Sugar Substitute. If fruit is reduced by half or more, no Low-Fructose Fruit servings should be tracked. Due to their extremely low sugar content, lemons should not be reduced and do not need to be tracked.

BLUEBERRY WHIRL

1 Serving   Prep: 1 min   Blend: 2 min   Total: 3 min
4 Non-Starchy Vegetables   1 Nutrient-Dense Protein   1 Low-Fructose Fruit

- 3/4 Cup Blueberries (frozen or fresh)
- 3 Cups Spinach
- 3 Cups Romaine Lettuce
- 1 Medium Lemon (peeled)
- 1/2 TSP Cinnamon
- 2 TBSP Garden in My Glass*
- 4 TBSP Clean Whey Protein**
- 1 TSP Hormone Healing Green Tea (optional)
- 2 TBSP Slimming Sugar Substitute (optional)***

DIRECTIONS

- Add all ingredients to a high-powered blender with 8 oz. cold water and a handful of ice.

- Blend for 2 minutes or until completely blended (i.e. no pieces of veggies or fruit are visible).

- Adjust the amount of water and ice for desired consistency and desired temperature.

TIP: Can't find some of these ingredients at your local grocery store? Have them delivered quickly and easily by visiting your SANE Superfoods Store at http://store.SANESolution.com.

NOTES

*You can add two additional serving of Non-Starchy Vegetables in place of the two tablespoons of Garden in My Glass. If you do not add more veggies and you do not add Garden in My Glass, track only two servings of Non-Starchy Vegetables per smoothie (instead of four servings).

**Only add protein if the smoothie is your entire meal. Vegetarians can use 6 TBSP of Clean Pea Protein (instead of Clean Whey Protein).

***To minimize sugar content, reduce fruit (other than lemon) and increase Slimming Sugar Substitute. If fruit is reduced by half or more, no Low-Fructose Fruit servings should be tracked. Due to their extremely low sugar content, lemons should not be reduced and do not need to be tracked.

CHERRY BREEZE

1 Serving   Prep: 1 min   Blend: 2 min   Total: 3 min
4 Non-Starchy Vegetables   1 Nutrient-Dense Protein   1 Low-Fructose Fruit

- 3/4 Cup Pitted Cherries (frozen or fresh)
- 2 Cups Kale
- 4 Cups Romaine Lettuce
- 1 Medium Lemon (peeled)
- 1/2 TSP Cinnamon
- 2 TBSP Garden in My Glass*
- 4 TBSP Clean Whey Protein**
- 1 TSP Hormone Healing Green Tea (optional)
- 2 TBSP Slimming Sugar Substitute (optional)***

DIRECTIONS

- Add all ingredients to a high-powered blender with 8 oz. cold water and a handful of ice.

- Blend for 2 minutes or until completely blended (i.e. no pieces of veggies or fruit are visible).

- Adjust the amount of water and ice for desired consistency and desired temperature.

TIP: Can't find some of these ingredients at your local grocery store? Have them delivered quickly and easily by visiting your SANE Superfoods Store at http://store.SANESolution.com.

NOTES

*You can add two additional serving of Non-Starchy Vegetables in place of the two tablespoons of Garden in My Glass. If you do not add more veggies and you do not add Garden in My Glass, track only two servings of Non-Starchy Vegetables per smoothie (instead of four servings).

**Only add protein if the smoothie is your entire meal. Vegetarians can use 6 TBSP of Clean Pea Protein (instead of Clean Whey Protein).

***To minimize sugar content, reduce fruit (other than lemon) and increase Slimming Sugar Substitute. If fruit is reduced by half or more, no Low-Fructose Fruit servings should be tracked. Due to their extremely low sugar content, lemons should not be reduced and do not need to be tracked.

CHERRY CRANBERRY BLAST

1 Serving   Prep: 1 min   Blend: 2 min   Total: 3 min
4 Non-Starchy Vegetables   1 Nutrient-Dense Protein   1 Low-Fructose Fruit

- 1/2 Cup Pitted Cherries (frozen or fresh)
- 1 Cup Pitted Cranberries (frozen or fresh)
- 6 Cups Spinach
- 1 Medium Lemon (peeled)
- 1/2 TSP Cinnamon
- 2 TBSP Garden in My Glass*
- 4 TBSP Clean Whey Protein**
- 1 TSP Hormone Healing Green Tea (optional)
- 2 TBSP Slimming Sugar Substitute (optional)***

DIRECTIONS

- Add all ingredients to a high-powered blender with 8 oz. cold water and a handful of ice.

- Blend for 2 minutes or until completely blended (i.e. no pieces of veggies or fruit are visible).

- Adjust the amount of water and ice for desired consistency and desired temperature.

TIP: Can't find some of these ingredients at your local grocery store? Have them delivered quickly and easily by visiting your SANE Superfoods Store at http://store.SANESolution.com.

NOTES

*You can add two additional serving of Non-Starchy Vegetables in place of the two tablespoons of Garden in My Glass. If you do not add more veggies and you do not add Garden in My Glass, track only two servings of Non-Starchy Vegetables per smoothie (instead of four servings).

**Only add protein if the smoothie is your entire meal. Vegetarians can use 6 TBSP of Clean Pea Protein (instead of Clean Whey Protein).

***To minimize sugar content, reduce fruit (other than lemon) and increase Slimming Sugar Substitute. If fruit is reduced by half or more, no Low-Fructose Fruit servings should be tracked. Due to their extremely low sugar content, lemons should not be reduced and do not need to be tracked.

CHERRY CRANBERRY BLISS

1 Serving   Prep: 1 min   Blend: 2 min   Total: 3 min
4 Non-Starchy Vegetables   1 Nutrient-Dense Protein   1 Low-Fructose Fruit

- 1/2 Cup Pitted Cherries (frozen or fresh)
- 1 Cup Pitted Cranberries (frozen or fresh)
- 2 Cups Arugula
- 4 Cups Romaine Lettuce
- 1 Medium Lemon (peeled)
- 1/2 TSP Cinnamon
- 2 TBSP Garden in My Glass*
- 4 TBSP Clean Whey Protein**
- 1 TSP Hormone Healing Green Tea (optional)
- 2 TBSP Slimming Sugar Substitute (optional)***

DIRECTIONS

- Add all ingredients to a high-powered blender with 8 oz. cold water and a handful of ice.

- Blend for 2 minutes or until completely blended (i.e. no pieces of veggies or fruit are visible).

- Adjust the amount of water and ice for desired consistency and desired temperature.

TIP: Can't find some of these ingredients at your local grocery store? Have them delivered quickly and easily by visiting your SANE Superfoods Store at http://store.SANESolution.com.

NOTES

*You can add two additional serving of Non-Starchy Vegetables in place of the two tablespoons of Garden in My Glass. If you do not add more veggies and you do not add Garden in My Glass, track only two servings of Non-Starchy Vegetables per smoothie (instead of four servings).

**Only add protein if the smoothie is your entire meal. Vegetarians can use 6 TBSP of Clean Pea Protein (instead of Clean Whey Protein).

***To minimize sugar content, reduce fruit (other than lemon) and increase Slimming Sugar Substitute. If fruit is reduced by half or more, no Low-Fructose Fruit servings should be tracked. Due to their extremely low sugar content, lemons should not be reduced and do not need to be tracked.

CHERRY CRANBERRY ESCAPE

1 Serving   Prep: 1 min   Blend: 2 min   Total: 3 min

4 Non-Starchy Vegetables   1 Nutrient-Dense Protein   1 Low-Fructose Fruit

- 1/2 Cup Pitted Cherries (frozen or fresh)
- 1 Cup Pitted Cranberries (frozen or fresh)
- 2 Cups Chard
- 4 Cups Spinach
- 1 Medium Lemon (peeled)
- 1/2 TSP Cinnamon
- 2 TBSP Garden in My Glass*
- 4 TBSP Clean Whey Protein**
- 1 TSP Hormone Healing Green Tea (optional)
- 2 TBSP Slimming Sugar Substitute (optional)***

DIRECTIONS

- Add all ingredients to a high-powered blender with 8 oz. cold water and a handful of ice.

- Blend for 2 minutes or until completely blended (i.e. no pieces of veggies or fruit are visible).

- Adjust the amount of water and ice for desired consistency and desired temperature.

TIP: Can't find some of these ingredients at your local grocery store? Have them delivered quickly and easily by visiting your SANE Superfoods Store at http://store.SANESolution.com.

NOTES

*You can add two additional serving of Non-Starchy Vegetables in place of the two tablespoons of Garden in My Glass. If you do not add more veggies and you do not add Garden in My Glass, track only two servings of Non-Starchy Vegetables per smoothie (instead of four servings).

**Only add protein if the smoothie is your entire meal. Vegetarians can use 6 TBSP of Clean Pea Protein (instead of Clean Whey Protein).

***To minimize sugar content, reduce fruit (other than lemon) and increase Slimming Sugar Substitute. If fruit is reduced by half or more, no Low-Fructose Fruit servings should be tracked. Due to their extremely low sugar content, lemons should not be reduced and do not need to be tracked.

CHERRY CRANBERRY GLEE

1 Serving   Prep: 1 min   Blend: 2 min   Total: 3 min

4 Non-Starchy Vegetables   1 Nutrient-Dense Protein   1 Low-Fructose Fruit

- 1/2 Cup Pitted Cherries (frozen or fresh)
- 1 Cup Pitted Cranberries (frozen or fresh)
- 2 Cups Chard
- 4 Cups Romaine Lettuce
- 1 Medium Lemon (peeled)
- 1/2 TSP Cinnamon
- 2 TBSP Garden in My Glass*
- 4 TBSP Clean Whey Protein**
- 1 TSP Hormone Healing Green Tea (optional)
- 2 TBSP Slimming Sugar Substitute (optional)***

DIRECTIONS

- Add all ingredients to a high-powered blender with 8 oz. cold water and a handful of ice.

- Blend for 2 minutes or until completely blended (i.e. no pieces of veggies or fruit are visible).

- Adjust the amount of water and ice for desired consistency and desired temperature.

TIP: Can't find some of these ingredients at your local grocery store? Have them delivered quickly and easily by visiting your SANE Superfoods Store at http://store.SANESolution.com.

NOTES

*You can add two additional serving of Non-Starchy Vegetables in place of the two tablespoons of Garden in My Glass. If you do not add more veggies and you do not add Garden in My Glass, track only two servings of Non-Starchy Vegetables per smoothie (instead of four servings).

**Only add protein if the smoothie is your entire meal. Vegetarians can use 6 TBSP of Clean Pea Protein (instead of Clean Whey Protein).

***To minimize sugar content, reduce fruit (other than lemon) and increase Slimming Sugar Substitute. If fruit is reduced by half or more, no Low-Fructose Fruit servings should be tracked. Due to their extremely low sugar content, lemons should not be reduced and do not need to be tracked.

CHERRY CRANBERRY MAGIC

1 Serving   Prep: 1 min   Blend: 2 min   Total: 3 min

4 Non-Starchy Vegetables   1 Nutrient-Dense Protein   1 Low-Fructose Fruit

- 1/2 Cup Pitted Cherries (frozen or fresh)
- 1 Cup Pitted Cranberries (frozen or fresh)
- 2 Cups Arugula
- 4 Cups Spinach
- 1 Medium Lemon (peeled)
- 1/2 TSP Cinnamon
- 2 TBSP Garden in My Glass*
- 4 TBSP Clean Whey Protein**
- 1 TSP Hormone Healing Green Tea (optional)
- 2 TBSP Slimming Sugar Substitute (optional)***

DIRECTIONS

- Add all ingredients to a high-powered blender with 8 oz. cold water and a handful of ice.

- Blend for 2 minutes or until completely blended (i.e. no pieces of veggies or fruit are visible).

- Adjust the amount of water and ice for desired consistency and desired temperature.

TIP: Can't find some of these ingredients at your local grocery store? Have them delivered quickly and easily by visiting your SANE Superfoods Store at http://store.SANESolution.com.

NOTES

*You can add two additional serving of Non-Starchy Vegetables in place of the two tablespoons of Garden in My Glass. If you do not add more veggies and you do not add Garden in My Glass, track only two servings of Non-Starchy Vegetables per smoothie (instead of four servings).

**Only add protein if the smoothie is your entire meal. Vegetarians can use 6 TBSP of Clean Pea Protein (instead of Clean Whey Protein).

***To minimize sugar content, reduce fruit (other than lemon) and increase Slimming Sugar Substitute. If fruit is reduced by half or more, no Low-Fructose Fruit servings should be tracked. Due to their extremely low sugar content, lemons should not be reduced and do not need to be tracked.

CHERRY ESCAPE

1 Serving   Prep: 1 min   Blend: 2 min   Total: 3 min
4 Non-Starchy Vegetables   1 Nutrient-Dense Protein   1 Low-Fructose Fruit

- 3/4 Cup Pitted Cherries (frozen or fresh)
- 2 Cups Chard
- 4 Cups Spinach
- 1 Medium Lemon (peeled)
- 1/2 TSP Cinnamon
- 2 TBSP Garden in My Glass*
- 4 TBSP Clean Whey Protein**
- 1 TSP Hormone Healing Green Tea (optional)
- 2 TBSP Slimming Sugar Substitute (optional)***

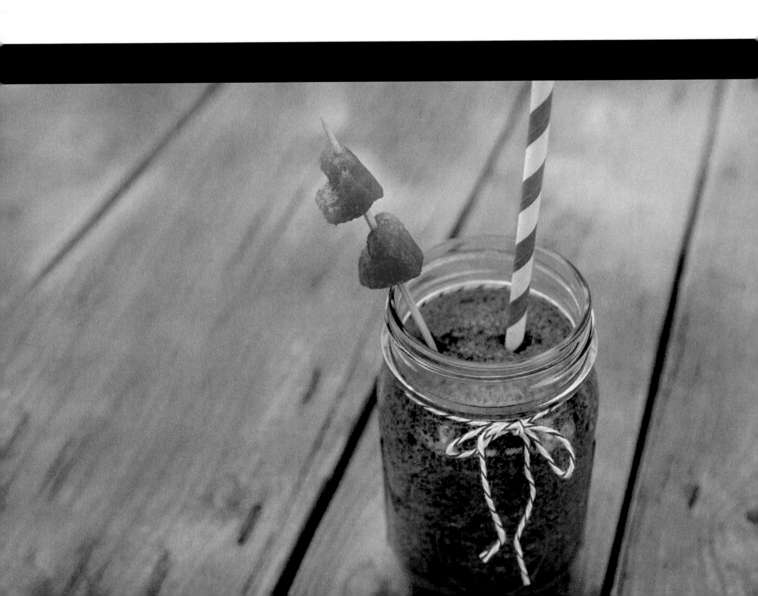

DIRECTIONS

- Add all ingredients to a high-powered blender with 8 oz. cold water and a handful of ice.

- Blend for 2 minutes or until completely blended (i.e. no pieces of veggies or fruit are visible).

- Adjust the amount of water and ice for desired consistency and desired temperature.

TIP: Can't find some of these ingredients at your local grocery store? Have them delivered quickly and easily by visiting your SANE Superfoods Store at http://store.SANESolution.com.

NOTES

*You can add two additional serving of Non-Starchy Vegetables in place of the two tablespoons of Garden in My Glass. If you do not add more veggies and you do not add Garden in My Glass, track only two servings of Non-Starchy Vegetables per smoothie (instead of four servings).

**Only add protein if the smoothie is your entire meal. Vegetarians can use 6 TBSP of Clean Pea Protein (instead of Clean Whey Protein).

***To minimize sugar content, reduce fruit (other than lemon) and increase Slimming Sugar Substitute. If fruit is reduced by half or more, no Low-Fructose Fruit servings should be tracked. Due to their extremely low sugar content, lemons should not be reduced and do not need to be tracked.

CHERRY SUNRISE

1 Serving   Prep: 1 min   Blend: 2 min   Total: 3 min
4 Non-Starchy Vegetables   1 Nutrient-Dense Protein   1 Low-Fructose Fruit

- 3/4 Cup Pitted Cherries (frozen or fresh)
- 6 Cups Romaine Lettuce
- 1 Medium Lemon (peeled)
- 1/2 TSP Cinnamon
- 2 TBSP Garden in My Glass*
- 4 TBSP Clean Whey Protein**
- 1 TSP Hormone Healing Green Tea (optional)
- 2 TBSP Slimming Sugar Substitute (optional)***

DIRECTIONS

- Add all ingredients to a high-powered blender with 8 oz. cold water and a handful of ice.

- Blend for 2 minutes or until completely blended (i.e. no pieces of veggies or fruit are visible).

- Adjust the amount of water and ice for desired consistency and desired temperature.

TIP: Can't find some of these ingredients at your local grocery store? Have them delivered quickly and easily by visiting your SANE Superfoods Store at http://store.SANESolution.com.

NOTES

*You can add two additional serving of Non-Starchy Vegetables in place of the two tablespoons of Garden in My Glass. If you do not add more veggies and you do not add Garden in My Glass, track only two servings of Non-Starchy Vegetables per smoothie (instead of four servings).

**Only add protein if the smoothie is your entire meal. Vegetarians can use 6 TBSP of Clean Pea Protein (instead of Clean Whey Protein).

***To minimize sugar content, reduce fruit (other than lemon) and increase Slimming Sugar Substitute. If fruit is reduced by half or more, no Low-Fructose Fruit servings should be tracked. Due to their extremely low sugar content, lemons should not be reduced and do not need to be tracked.

CRANBERRY BLUEBERRY BLISS

1 Serving   Prep: 1 min   Blend: 2 min   Total: 3 min
4 Non-Starchy Vegetables   1 Nutrient-Dense Protein   1 Low-Fructose Fruit

- 1 Cup Pitted Cranberries (frozen or fresh)
- 1/3 Cup Blueberries (frozen or fresh)
- 2 Cups Arugula
- 4 Cups Romaine Lettuce
- 1 Medium Lemon (peeled)
- 1/2 TSP Cinnamon
- 2 TBSP Garden in My Glass*
- 4 TBSP Clean Whey Protein**
- 1 TSP Hormone Healing Green Tea (optional)
- 2 TBSP Slimming Sugar Substitute (optional)***

DIRECTIONS

- Add all ingredients to a high-powered blender with 8 oz. cold water and a handful of ice.

- Blend for 2 minutes or until completely blended (i.e. no pieces of veggies or fruit are visible).

- Adjust the amount of water and ice for desired consistency and desired temperature.

TIP: Can't find some of these ingredients at your local grocery store? Have them delivered quickly and easily by visiting your SANE Superfoods Store at http://store.SANESolution.com.

NOTES

*You can add two additional serving of Non-Starchy Vegetables in place of the two tablespoons of Garden in My Glass. If you do not add more veggies and you do not add Garden in My Glass, track only two servings of Non-Starchy Vegetables per smoothie (instead of four servings).

**Only add protein if the smoothie is your entire meal. Vegetarians can use 6 TBSP of Clean Pea Protein (instead of Clean Whey Protein).

***To minimize sugar content, reduce fruit (other than lemon) and increase Slimming Sugar Substitute. If fruit is reduced by half or more, no Low-Fructose Fruit servings should be tracked. Due to their extremely low sugar content, lemons should not be reduced and do not need to be tracked.

CRANBERRY BLUEBERRY DREAM

1 Serving   Prep: 1 min   Blend: 2 min   Total: 3 min
4 Non-Starchy Vegetables   1 Nutrient-Dense Protein   1 Low-Fructose Fruit

- 1 Cup Pitted Cranberries (frozen or fresh)
- 1/3 Cup Blueberries (frozen or fresh)
- 3 Cups Mixed Greens
- 3 Cups Spinach
- 1 Medium Lemon (peeled)
- 1/2 TSP Cinnamon
- 2 TBSP Garden in My Glass*
- 4 TBSP Clean Whey Protein**
- 1 TSP Hormone Healing Green Tea (optional)
- 2 TBSP Slimming Sugar Substitute (optional)***

DIRECTIONS

- Add all ingredients to a high-powered blender with 8 oz. cold water and a handful of ice.

- Blend for 2 minutes or until completely blended (i.e. no pieces of veggies or fruit are visible).

- Adjust the amount of water and ice for desired consistency and desired temperature.

TIP: Can't find some of these ingredients at your local grocery store? Have them delivered quickly and easily by visiting your SANE Superfoods Store at http://store.SANESolution.com.

NOTES

*You can add two additional serving of Non-Starchy Vegetables in place of the two tablespoons of Garden in My Glass. If you do not add more veggies and you do not add Garden in My Glass, track only two servings of Non-Starchy Vegetables per smoothie (instead of four servings).

**Only add protein if the smoothie is your entire meal. Vegetarians can use 6 TBSP of Clean Pea Protein (instead of Clean Whey Protein).

***To minimize sugar content, reduce fruit (other than lemon) and increase Slimming Sugar Substitute. If fruit is reduced by half or more, no Low-Fructose Fruit servings should be tracked. Due to their extremely low sugar content, lemons should not be reduced and do not need to be tracked.

CRANBERRY BLUEBERRY SUNRISE

1 Serving   Prep: 1 min   Blend: 2 min   Total: 3 min
4 Non-Starchy Vegetables   1 Nutrient-Dense Protein   1 Low-Fructose Fruit

- 1 Cup Pitted Cranberries (frozen or fresh)
- 1/3 Cup Blueberries (frozen or fresh)
- 6 Cups Romaine Lettuce
- 1 Medium Lemon (peeled)
- 1/2 TSP Cinnamon
- 2 TBSP Garden in My Glass*
- 4 TBSP Clean Whey Protein**
- 1 TSP Hormone Healing Green Tea (optional)
- 2 TBSP Slimming Sugar Substitute (optional)***

DIRECTIONS

- Add all ingredients to a high-powered blender with 8 oz. cold water and a handful of ice.

- Blend for 2 minutes or until completely blended (i.e. no pieces of veggies or fruit are visible).

- Adjust the amount of water and ice for desired consistency and desired temperature.

TIP: Can't find some of these ingredients at your local grocery store? Have them delivered quickly and easily by visiting your SANE Superfoods Store at http://store.SANESolution.com.

NOTES

*You can add two additional serving of Non-Starchy Vegetables in place of the two tablespoons of Garden in My Glass. If you do not add more veggies and you do not add Garden in My Glass, track only two servings of Non-Starchy Vegetables per smoothie (instead of four servings).

**Only add protein if the smoothie is your entire meal. Vegetarians can use 6 TBSP of Clean Pea Protein (instead of Clean Whey Protein).

***To minimize sugar content, reduce fruit (other than lemon) and increase Slimming Sugar Substitute. If fruit is reduced by half or more, no Low-Fructose Fruit servings should be tracked. Due to their extremely low sugar content, lemons should not be reduced and do not need to be tracked.

CRANBERRY BREEZE

1 Serving   Prep: 1 min   Blend: 2 min   Total: 3 min
4 Non-Starchy Vegetables   1 Nutrient-Dense Protein   1 Low-Fructose Fruit

- 1 1/2 Cups Pitted Cranberries (frozen or fresh)
- 2 Cups Kale
- 4 Cups Romaine Lettuce
- 1 Medium Lemon (peeled)
- 1/2 TSP Cinnamon
- 2 TBSP Garden in My Glass*
- 4 TBSP Clean Whey Protein**
- 1 TSP Hormone Healing Green Tea (optional)
- 2 TBSP Slimming Sugar Substitute (optional)***

DIRECTIONS

- Add all ingredients to a high-powered blender with 8 oz. cold water and a handful of ice.

- Blend for 2 minutes or until completely blended (i.e. no pieces of veggies or fruit are visible).

- Adjust the amount of water and ice for desired consistency and desired temperature.

TIP: Can't find some of these ingredients at your local grocery store? Have them delivered quickly and easily by visiting your SANE Superfoods Store at http://store.SANESolution.com.

NOTES

*You can add two additional serving of Non-Starchy Vegetables in place of the two tablespoons of Garden in My Glass. If you do not add more veggies and you do not add Garden in My Glass, track only two servings of Non-Starchy Vegetables per smoothie (instead of four servings).

**Only add protein if the smoothie is your entire meal. Vegetarians can use 6 TBSP of Clean Pea Protein (instead of Clean Whey Protein).

***To minimize sugar content, reduce fruit (other than lemon) and increase Slimming Sugar Substitute. If fruit is reduced by half or more, no Low-Fructose Fruit servings should be tracked. Due to their extremely low sugar content, lemons should not be reduced and do not need to be tracked.

CRANBERRY DELIGHT

1 Serving   Prep: 1 min   Blend: 2 min   Total: 3 min
4 Non-Starchy Vegetables   1 Nutrient-Dense Protein   1 Low-Fructose Fruit

- 1 1/2 Cups Pitted Cranberries (frozen or fresh)
- 2 Cups Kale
- 4 Cups Spinach
- 1 Medium Lemon (peeled)
- 1/2 TSP Cinnamon
- 2 TBSP Garden in My Glass*
- 4 TBSP Clean Whey Protein**
- 1 TSP Hormone Healing Green Tea (optional)
- 2 TBSP Slimming Sugar Substitute (optional)***

DIRECTIONS

- Add all ingredients to a high-powered blender with 8 oz. cold water and a handful of ice.

- Blend for 2 minutes or until completely blended (i.e. no pieces of veggies or fruit are visible).

- Adjust the amount of water and ice for desired consistency and desired temperature.

TIP: Can't find some of these ingredients at your local grocery store? Have them delivered quickly and easily by visiting your SANE Superfoods Store at http://store.SANESolution.com.

NOTES

*You can add two additional serving of Non-Starchy Vegetables in place of the two tablespoons of Garden in My Glass. If you do not add more veggies and you do not add Garden in My Glass, track only two servings of Non-Starchy Vegetables per smoothie (instead of four servings).

**Only add protein if the smoothie is your entire meal. Vegetarians can use 6 TBSP of Clean Pea Protein (instead of Clean Whey Protein).

***To minimize sugar content, reduce fruit (other than lemon) and increase Slimming Sugar Substitute. If fruit is reduced by half or more, no Low-Fructose Fruit servings should be tracked. Due to their extremely low sugar content, lemons should not be reduced and do not need to be tracked.

CRANBERRY GLEE

1 Serving   Prep: 1 min   Blend: 2 min   Total: 3 min
4 Non-Starchy Vegetables   1 Nutrient-Dense Protein   1 Low-Fructose Fruit

- 1 1/2 Cups Pitted Cranberries (frozen or fresh)
- 2 Cups Chard
- 4 Cups Romaine Lettuce
- 1 Medium Lemon (peeled)
- 1/2 TSP Cinnamon
- 2 TBSP Garden in My Glass*
- 4 TBSP Clean Whey Protein**
- 1 TSP Hormone Healing Green Tea (optional)
- 2 TBSP Slimming Sugar Substitute (optional)***

DIRECTIONS

- Add all ingredients to a high-powered blender with 8 oz. cold water and a handful of ice.

- Blend for 2 minutes or until completely blended (i.e. no pieces of veggies or fruit are visible).

- Adjust the amount of water and ice for desired consistency and desired temperature.

TIP: Can't find some of these ingredients at your local grocery store? Have them delivered quickly and easily by visiting your SANE Superfoods Store at http://store.SANESolution.com.

NOTES

*You can add two additional serving of Non-Starchy Vegetables in place of the two tablespoons of Garden in My Glass. If you do not add more veggies and you do not add Garden in My Glass, track only two servings of Non-Starchy Vegetables per smoothie (instead of four servings).

**Only add protein if the smoothie is your entire meal. Vegetarians can use 6 TBSP of Clean Pea Protein (instead of Clean Whey Protein).

***To minimize sugar content, reduce fruit (other than lemon) and increase Slimming Sugar Substitute. If fruit is reduced by half or more, no Low-Fructose Fruit servings should be tracked. Due to their extremely low sugar content, lemons should not be reduced and do not need to be tracked.

CRANBERRY GRAPEFRUIT BREEZE

1 Serving   Prep: 1 min   Blend: 2 min   Total: 3 min
4 Non-Starchy Vegetables   1 Nutrient-Dense Protein   1 Low-Fructose Fruit

- 1 Cup Pitted Cranberries (frozen or fresh)
- 1/2 Medium Grapefruit (peeled)
- 2 Cups Kale
- 4 Cups Romaine Lettuce
- 1 Medium Lemon (peeled)
- 1/2 TSP Cinnamon
- 2 TBSP Garden in My Glass*
- 4 TBSP Clean Whey Protein**
- 1 TSP Hormone Healing Green Tea (optional)
- 2 TBSP Slimming Sugar Substitute (optional)***

DIRECTIONS

- Add all ingredients to a high-powered blender with 8 oz. cold water and a handful of ice.

- Blend for 2 minutes or until completely blended (i.e. no pieces of veggies or fruit are visible).

- Adjust the amount of water and ice for desired consistency and desired temperature.

TIP: Can't find some of these ingredients at your local grocery store? Have them delivered quickly and easily by visiting your SANE Superfoods Store at http://store.SANESolution.com.

NOTES

*You can add two additional serving of Non-Starchy Vegetables in place of the two tablespoons of Garden in My Glass. If you do not add more veggies and you do not add Garden in My Glass, track only two servings of Non-Starchy Vegetables per smoothie (instead of four servings).

**Only add protein if the smoothie is your entire meal. Vegetarians can use 6 TBSP of Clean Pea Protein (instead of Clean Whey Protein).

***To minimize sugar content, reduce fruit (other than lemon) and increase Slimming Sugar Substitute. If fruit is reduced by half or more, no Low-Fructose Fruit servings should be tracked. Due to their extremely low sugar content, lemons should not be reduced and do not need to be tracked.

CRANBERRY GRAPEFRUIT DREAM

1 Serving   Prep: 1 min   Blend: 2 min   Total: 3 min
4 Non-Starchy Vegetables   1 Nutrient-Dense Protein   1 Low-Fructose Fruit

- 1 Cup Pitted Cranberries (frozen or fresh)
- 1/2 Medium Grapefruit (peeled)
- 3 Cups Mixed Greens
- 3 Cups Spinach
- 1 Medium Lemon (peeled)
- 1/2 TSP Cinnamon
- 2 TBSP Garden in My Glass*
- 4 TBSP Clean Whey Protein**
- 1 TSP Hormone Healing Green Tea (optional)
- 2 TBSP Slimming Sugar Substitute (optional)***

DIRECTIONS

- Add all ingredients to a high-powered blender with 8 oz. cold water and a handful of ice.

- Blend for 2 minutes or until completely blended (i.e. no pieces of veggies or fruit are visible).

- Adjust the amount of water and ice for desired consistency and desired temperature.

TIP: Can't find some of these ingredients at your local grocery store? Have them delivered quickly and easily by visiting your SANE Superfoods Store at http://store.SANESolution.com.

NOTES

*You can add two additional serving of Non-Starchy Vegetables in place of the two tablespoons of Garden in My Glass. If you do not add more veggies and you do not add Garden in My Glass, track only two servings of Non-Starchy Vegetables per smoothie (instead of four servings).

**Only add protein if the smoothie is your entire meal. Vegetarians can use 6 TBSP of Clean Pea Protein (instead of Clean Whey Protein).

***To minimize sugar content, reduce fruit (other than lemon) and increase Slimming Sugar Substitute. If fruit is reduced by half or more, no Low-Fructose Fruit servings should be tracked. Due to their extremely low sugar content, lemons should not be reduced and do not need to be tracked.

CRANBERRY GRAPEFRUIT ESCAPE

1 Serving   Prep: 1 min   Blend: 2 min   Total: 3 min
4 Non-Starchy Vegetables   1 Nutrient-Dense Protein   1 Low-Fructose Fruit

- 1 Cup Pitted Cranberries (frozen or fresh)
- 1/2 Medium Grapefruit (peeled)
- 2 Cups Chard
- 4 Cups Spinach
- 1 Medium Lemon (peeled)
- 1/2 TSP Cinnamon
- 2 TBSP Garden in My Glass*
- 4 TBSP Clean Whey Protein**
- 1 TSP Hormone Healing Green Tea (optional)
- 2 TBSP Slimming Sugar Substitute (optional)***

Directions

- Add all ingredients to a high-powered blender with 8 oz. cold water and a handful of ice.

- Blend for 2 minutes or until completely blended (i.e. no pieces of veggies or fruit are visible).

- Adjust the amount of water and ice for desired consistency and desired temperature.

TIP: Can't find some of these ingredients at your local grocery store? Have them delivered quickly and easily by visiting your SANE Superfoods Store at http://store.SANESolution.com.

Notes

*You can add two additional serving of Non-Starchy Vegetables in place of the two tablespoons of Garden in My Glass. If you do not add more veggies and you do not add Garden in My Glass, track only two servings of Non-Starchy Vegetables per smoothie (instead of four servings).

**Only add protein if the smoothie is your entire meal. Vegetarians can use 6 TBSP of Clean Pea Protein (instead of Clean Whey Protein).

***To minimize sugar content, reduce fruit (other than lemon) and increase Slimming Sugar Substitute. If fruit is reduced by half or more, no Low-Fructose Fruit servings should be tracked. Due to their extremely low sugar content, lemons should not be reduced and do not need to be tracked.

CRANBERRY GRAPEFRUIT SUNRISE

1 Serving   Prep: 1 min   Blend: 2 min   Total: 3 min
4 Non-Starchy Vegetables   1 Nutrient-Dense Protein   1 Low-Fructose Fruit

- 1 Cup Pitted Cranberries (frozen or fresh)
- 1/2 Medium Grapefruit (peeled)
- 6 Cups Romaine Lettuce
- 1 Medium Lemon (peeled)
- 1/2 TSP Cinnamon
- 2 TBSP Garden in My Glass*
- 4 TBSP Clean Whey Protein**
- 1 TSP Hormone Healing Green Tea (optional)
- 2 TBSP Slimming Sugar Substitute (optional)***

DIRECTIONS

- Add all ingredients to a high-powered blender with 8 oz. cold water and a handful of ice.

- Blend for 2 minutes or until completely blended (i.e. no pieces of veggies or fruit are visible).

- Adjust the amount of water and ice for desired consistency and desired temperature.

TIP: Can't find some of these ingredients at your local grocery store? Have them delivered quickly and easily by visiting your SANE Superfoods Store at http://store.SANESolution.com.

NOTES

*You can add two additional serving of Non-Starchy Vegetables in place of the two tablespoons of Garden in My Glass. If you do not add more veggies and you do not add Garden in My Glass, track only two servings of Non-Starchy Vegetables per smoothie (instead of four servings).

**Only add protein if the smoothie is your entire meal. Vegetarians can use 6 TBSP of Clean Pea Protein (instead of Clean Whey Protein).

***To minimize sugar content, reduce fruit (other than lemon) and increase Slimming Sugar Substitute. If fruit is reduced by half or more, no Low-Fructose Fruit servings should be tracked. Due to their extremely low sugar content, lemons should not be reduced and do not need to be tracked.

CRANBERRY ORANGE BLISS

1 Serving   Prep: 1 min   Blend: 2 min   Total: 3 min
4 Non-Starchy Vegetables   1 Nutrient-Dense Protein   1 Low-Fructose Fruit

- 1 Cup Pitted Cranberries (frozen or fresh)
- 1/2 Medium Orange (peeled)
- 2 Cups Arugula
- 4 Cups Romaine Lettuce
- 1 Medium Lemon (peeled)
- 1/2 TSP Cinnamon
- 2 TBSP Garden in My Glass*
- 4 TBSP Clean Whey Protein**
- 1 TSP Hormone Healing Green Tea (optional)
- 2 TBSP Slimming Sugar Substitute (optional)***

DIRECTIONS

- Add all ingredients to a high-powered blender with 8 oz. cold water and a handful of ice.

- Blend for 2 minutes or until completely blended (i.e. no pieces of veggies or fruit are visible).

- Adjust the amount of water and ice for desired consistency and desired temperature.

TIP: Can't find some of these ingredients at your local grocery store? Have them delivered quickly and easily by visiting your SANE Superfoods Store at http://store.SANESolution.com.

NOTES

*You can add two additional serving of Non-Starchy Vegetables in place of the two tablespoons of Garden in My Glass. If you do not add more veggies and you do not add Garden in My Glass, track only two servings of Non-Starchy Vegetables per smoothie (instead of four servings).

**Only add protein if the smoothie is your entire meal. Vegetarians can use 6 TBSP of Clean Pea Protein (instead of Clean Whey Protein).

***To minimize sugar content, reduce fruit (other than lemon) and increase Slimming Sugar Substitute. If fruit is reduced by half or more, no Low-Fructose Fruit servings should be tracked. Due to their extremely low sugar content, lemons should not be reduced and do not need to be tracked.

CRANBERRY ORANGE DREAM

1 Serving   Prep: 1 min   Blend: 2 min   Total: 3 min

4 Non-Starchy Vegetables   1 Nutrient-Dense Protein   1 Low-Fructose Fruit

- 1 Cup Pitted Cranberries (frozen or fresh)
- 1/2 Medium Orange (peeled)
- 3 Cups Mixed Greens
- 3 Cups Spinach
- 1 Medium Lemon (peeled)
- 1/2 TSP Cinnamon
- 2 TBSP Garden in My Glass*
- 4 TBSP Clean Whey Protein**
- 1 TSP Hormone Healing Green Tea (optional)
- 2 TBSP Slimming Sugar Substitute (optional)***

DIRECTIONS

- Add all ingredients to a high-powered blender with 8 oz. cold water and a handful of ice.

- Blend for 2 minutes or until completely blended (i.e. no pieces of veggies or fruit are visible).

- Adjust the amount of water and ice for desired consistency and desired temperature.

TIP: Can't find some of these ingredients at your local grocery store? Have them delivered quickly and easily by visiting your SANE Superfoods Store at http://store.SANESolution.com.

NOTES

*You can add two additional serving of Non-Starchy Vegetables in place of the two tablespoons of Garden in My Glass. If you do not add more veggies and you do not add Garden in My Glass, track only two servings of Non-Starchy Vegetables per smoothie (instead of four servings).

**Only add protein if the smoothie is your entire meal. Vegetarians can use 6 TBSP of Clean Pea Protein (instead of Clean Whey Protein).

***To minimize sugar content, reduce fruit (other than lemon) and increase Slimming Sugar Substitute. If fruit is reduced by half or more, no Low-Fructose Fruit servings should be tracked. Due to their extremely low sugar content, lemons should not be reduced and do not need to be tracked.

CRANBERRY ORANGE ESCAPE

1 Serving   Prep: 1 min   Blend: 2 min   Total: 3 min
4 Non-Starchy Vegetables   1 Nutrient-Dense Protein   1 Low-Fructose Fruit

- 1 Cup Pitted Cranberries (frozen or fresh)
- 1/2 Medium Orange
- 2 Cups Chard
- 4 Cups Spinach
- 1 Medium Lemon (peeled)
- 1/2 TSP Cinnamon
- 2 TBSP Garden in My Glass*
- 4 TBSP Clean Whey Protein**
- 1 TSP Hormone Healing Green Tea (optional)
- 2 TBSP Slimming Sugar Substitute (optional)***

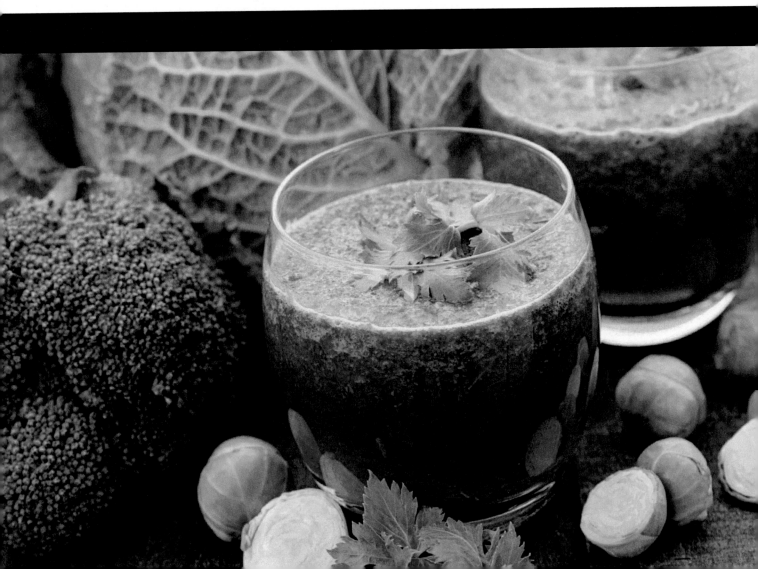

DIRECTIONS

- Add all ingredients to a high-powered blender with 8 oz. cold water and a handful of ice.

- Blend for 2 minutes or until completely blended (i.e. no pieces of veggies or fruit are visible).

- Adjust the amount of water and ice for desired consistency and desired temperature.

TIP: Can't find some of these ingredients at your local grocery store? Have them delivered quickly and easily by visiting your SANE Superfoods Store at http://store.SANESolution.com.

NOTES

*You can add two additional serving of Non-Starchy Vegetables in place of the two tablespoons of Garden in My Glass. If you do not add more veggies and you do not add Garden in My Glass, track only two servings of Non-Starchy Vegetables per smoothie (instead of four servings).

**Only add protein if the smoothie is your entire meal. Vegetarians can use 6 TBSP of Clean Pea Protein (instead of Clean Whey Protein).

***To minimize sugar content, reduce fruit (other than lemon) and increase Slimming Sugar Substitute. If fruit is reduced by half or more, no Low-Fructose Fruit servings should be tracked. Due to their extremely low sugar content, lemons should not be reduced and do not need to be tracked.

CRANBERRY PEACH BLISS

1 Serving   Prep: 1 min   Blend: 2 min   Total: 3 min
4 Non-Starchy Vegetables   1 Nutrient-Dense Protein   1 Low-Fructose Fruit

- 1 Cup Pitted Cranberries (frozen or fresh)
- 1/2 Cup Peach Slices (frozen or fresh)
- 2 Cups Arugula
- 4 Cups Romaine Lettuce
- 1 Medium Lemon (peeled)
- 1/2 TSP Cinnamon
- 2 TBSP Garden in My Glass*
- 4 TBSP Clean Whey Protein**
- 1 TSP Hormone Healing Green Tea (optional)
- 2 TBSP Slimming Sugar Substitute (optional)***

DIRECTIONS

- Add all ingredients to a high-powered blender with 8 oz. cold water and a handful of ice.

- Blend for 2 minutes or until completely blended (i.e. no pieces of veggies or fruit are visible).

- Adjust the amount of water and ice for desired consistency and desired temperature.

TIP: Can't find some of these ingredients at your local grocery store? Have them delivered quickly and easily by visiting your SANE Superfoods Store at http://store.SANESolution.com.

NOTES

*You can add two additional serving of Non-Starchy Vegetables in place of the two tablespoons of Garden in My Glass. If you do not add more veggies and you do not add Garden in My Glass, track only two servings of Non-Starchy Vegetables per smoothie (instead of four servings).

**Only add protein if the smoothie is your entire meal. Vegetarians can use 6 TBSP of Clean Pea Protein (instead of Clean Whey Protein).

***To minimize sugar content, reduce fruit (other than lemon) and increase Slimming Sugar Substitute. If fruit is reduced by half or more, no Low-Fructose Fruit servings should be tracked. Due to their extremely low sugar content, lemons should not be reduced and do not need to be tracked.

CRANBERRY PEACH DREAM

1 Serving   Prep: 1 min   Blend: 2 min   Total: 3 min
4 Non-Starchy Vegetables   1 Nutrient-Dense Protein   1 Low-Fructose Fruit

- 1 Cup Pitted Cranberries (frozen or fresh)
- 1/2 Cup Peach Slices (frozen or fresh)
- 3 Cups Mixed Greens
- 3 Cups Spinach
- 1 Medium Lemon (peeled)
- 1/2 TSP Cinnamon
- 2 TBSP Garden in My Glass*
- 4 TBSP Clean Whey Protein**
- 1 TSP Hormone Healing Green Tea (optional)
- 2 TBSP Slimming Sugar Substitute (optional)***

DIRECTIONS

- Add all ingredients to a high-powered blender with 8 oz. cold water and a handful of ice.

- Blend for 2 minutes or until completely blended (i.e. no pieces of veggies or fruit are visible).

- Adjust the amount of water and ice for desired consistency and desired temperature.

TIP: Can't find some of these ingredients at your local grocery store? Have them delivered quickly and easily by visiting your SANE Superfoods Store at http://store.SANESolution.com.

NOTES

*You can add two additional serving of Non-Starchy Vegetables in place of the two tablespoons of Garden in My Glass. If you do not add more veggies and you do not add Garden in My Glass, track only two servings of Non-Starchy Vegetables per smoothie (instead of four servings).

**Only add protein if the smoothie is your entire meal. Vegetarians can use 6 TBSP of Clean Pea Protein (instead of Clean Whey Protein).

***To minimize sugar content, reduce fruit (other than lemon) and increase Slimming Sugar Substitute. If fruit is reduced by half or more, no Low-Fructose Fruit servings should be tracked. Due to their extremely low sugar content, lemons should not be reduced and do not need to be tracked.

CRANBERRY PEACH GLEE

1 Serving   Prep: 1 min   Blend: 2 min   Total: 3 min
4 Non-Starchy Vegetables   1 Nutrient-Dense Protein   1 Low-Fructose Fruit

- 1 Cup Pitted Cranberries (frozen or fresh)
- 1/2 Cup Peach Slices (frozen or fresh)
- 2 Cups Chard
- 4 Cups Romaine Lettuce
- 1 Medium Lemon (peeled)
- 1/2 TSP Cinnamon
- 2 TBSP Garden in My Glass*
- 4 TBSP Clean Whey Protein**
- 1 TSP Hormone Healing Green Tea (optional)
- 2 TBSP Slimming Sugar Substitute (optional)***

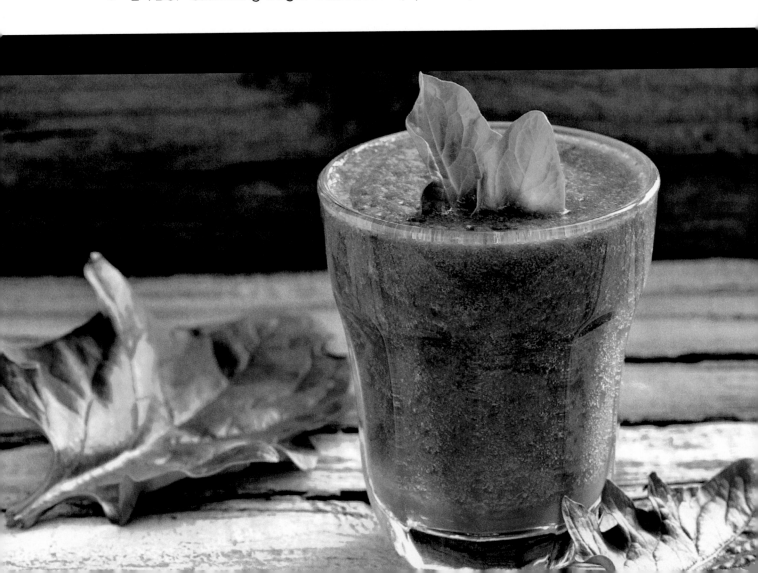

DIRECTIONS

- Add all ingredients to a high-powered blender with 8 oz. cold water and a handful of ice.

- Blend for 2 minutes or until completely blended (i.e. no pieces of veggies or fruit are visible).

- Adjust the amount of water and ice for desired consistency and desired temperature.

TIP: Can't find some of these ingredients at your local grocery store? Have them delivered quickly and easily by visiting your SANE Superfoods Store at http://store.SANESolution.com.

NOTES

*You can add two additional serving of Non-Starchy Vegetables in place of the two tablespoons of Garden in My Glass. If you do not add more veggies and you do not add Garden in My Glass, track only two servings of Non-Starchy Vegetables per smoothie (instead of four servings).

**Only add protein if the smoothie is your entire meal. Vegetarians can use 6 TBSP of Clean Pea Protein (instead of Clean Whey Protein).

***To minimize sugar content, reduce fruit (other than lemon) and increase Slimming Sugar Substitute. If fruit is reduced by half or more, no Low-Fructose Fruit servings should be tracked. Due to their extremely low sugar content, lemons should not be reduced and do not need to be tracked.

CRANBERRY PEACH SUNRISE

1 Serving   Prep: 1 min   Blend: 2 min   Total: 3 min
4 Non-Starchy Vegetables   1 Nutrient-Dense Protein   1 Low-Fructose Fruit

- 1 Cup Pitted Cranberries (frozen or fresh)
- 1/2 Cup Peach Slices (frozen or fresh)
- 6 Cups Romaine Lettuce
- 1 Medium Lemon (peeled)
- 1/2 TSP Cinnamon
- 2 TBSP Garden in My Glass*
- 4 TBSP Clean Whey Protein**
- 1 TSP Hormone Healing Green Tea (optional)
- 2 TBSP Slimming Sugar Substitute (optional)***

DIRECTIONS

- Add all ingredients to a high-powered blender with 8 oz. cold water and a handful of ice.

- Blend for 2 minutes or until completely blended (i.e. no pieces of veggies or fruit are visible).

- Adjust the amount of water and ice for desired consistency and desired temperature.

TIP: Can't find some of these ingredients at your local grocery store? Have them delivered quickly and easily by visiting your SANE Superfoods Store at http://store.SANESolution.com.

NOTES

*You can add two additional serving of Non-Starchy Vegetables in place of the two tablespoons of Garden in My Glass. If you do not add more veggies and you do not add Garden in My Glass, track only two servings of Non-Starchy Vegetables per smoothie (instead of four servings).

**Only add protein if the smoothie is your entire meal. Vegetarians can use 6 TBSP of Clean Pea Protein (instead of Clean Whey Protein).

***To minimize sugar content, reduce fruit (other than lemon) and increase Slimming Sugar Substitute. If fruit is reduced by half or more, no Low-Fructose Fruit servings should be tracked. Due to their extremely low sugar content, lemons should not be reduced and do not need to be tracked.

CRANBERRY PEACH WHIRL

1 Serving   Prep: 1 min   Blend: 2 min   Total: 3 min
4 Non-Starchy Vegetables   1 Nutrient-Dense Protein   1 Low-Fructose Fruit

- 1 Cup Pitted Cranberries (frozen or fresh)
- 1/2 Cup Peach Slices (frozen or fresh)
- 3 Cups Spinach
- 3 Cups Romaine Lettuce
- 1 Medium Lemon (peeled)
- 1/2 TSP Cinnamon
- 2 TBSP Garden in My Glass*
- 4 TBSP Clean Whey Protein**
- 1 TSP Hormone Healing Green Tea (optional)
- 2 TBSP Slimming Sugar Substitute (optional)***

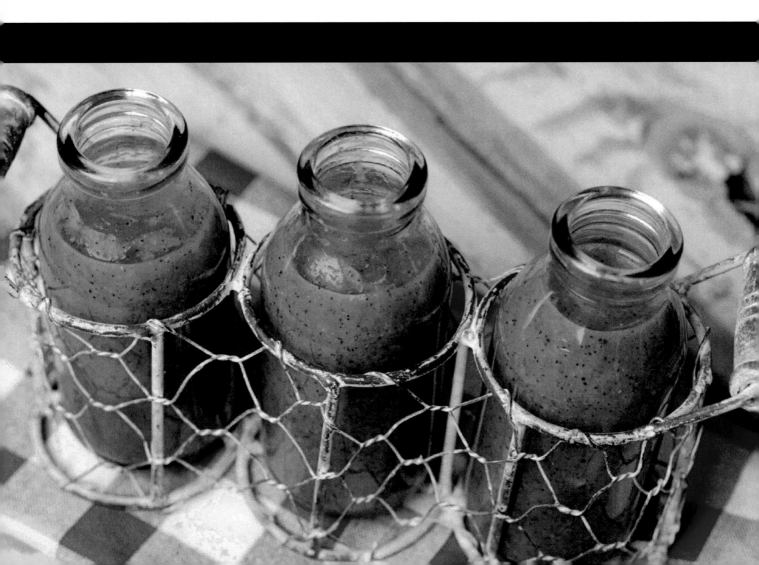

DIRECTIONS

- Add all ingredients to a high-powered blender with 8 oz. cold water and a handful of ice.

- Blend for 2 minutes or until completely blended (i.e. no pieces of veggies or fruit are visible).

- Adjust the amount of water and ice for desired consistency and desired temperature.

TIP: Can't find some of these ingredients at your local grocery store? Have them delivered quickly and easily by visiting your SANE Superfoods Store at http://store.SANESolution.com.

NOTES

*You can add two additional serving of Non-Starchy Vegetables in place of the two tablespoons of Garden in My Glass. If you do not add more veggies and you do not add Garden in My Glass, track only two servings of Non-Starchy Vegetables per smoothie (instead of four servings).

**Only add protein if the smoothie is your entire meal. Vegetarians can use 6 TBSP of Clean Pea Protein (instead of Clean Whey Protein).

***To minimize sugar content, reduce fruit (other than lemon) and increase Slimming Sugar Substitute. If fruit is reduced by half or more, no Low-Fructose Fruit servings should be tracked. Due to their extremely low sugar content, lemons should not be reduced and do not need to be tracked.

CRANBERRY STRAWBERRY BLAST

1 Serving   Prep: 1 min   Blend: 2 min   Total: 3 min
4 Non-Starchy Vegetables   1 Nutrient-Dense Protein   1 Low-Fructose Fruit

- 1 Cup Pitted Cranberries (frozen or fresh)
- 1/2 Cup Strawberries (frozen or fresh)
- 6 Cups Spinach
- 1 Medium Lemon (peeled)
- 1/2 TSP Cinnamon
- 2 TBSP Garden in My Glass*
- 4 TBSP Clean Whey Protein**
- 1 TSP Hormone Healing Green Tea (optional)
- 2 TBSP Slimming Sugar Substitute (optional)***

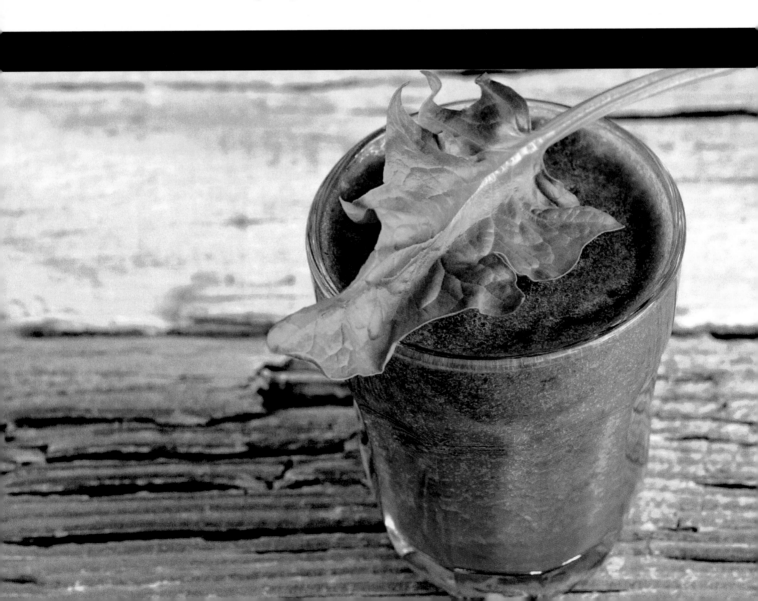

DIRECTIONS

- Add all ingredients to a high-powered blender with 8 oz. cold water and a handful of ice.

- Blend for 2 minutes or until completely blended (i.e. no pieces of veggies or fruit are visible).

- Adjust the amount of water and ice for desired consistency and desired temperature.

TIP: Can't find some of these ingredients at your local grocery store? Have them delivered quickly and easily by visiting your SANE Superfoods Store at http://store.SANESolution.com.

NOTES

*You can add two additional serving of Non-Starchy Vegetables in place of the two tablespoons of Garden in My Glass. If you do not add more veggies and you do not add Garden in My Glass, track only two servings of Non-Starchy Vegetables per smoothie (instead of four servings).

**Only add protein if the smoothie is your entire meal. Vegetarians can use 6 TBSP of Clean Pea Protein (instead of Clean Whey Protein).

***To minimize sugar content, reduce fruit (other than lemon) and increase Slimming Sugar Substitute. If fruit is reduced by half or more, no Low-Fructose Fruit servings should be tracked. Due to their extremely low sugar content, lemons should not be reduced and do not need to be tracked.

CRANBERRY STRAWBERRY DELIGHT

1 Serving   Prep: 1 min   Blend: 2 min   Total: 3 min
4 Non-Starchy Vegetables   1 Nutrient-Dense Protein   1 Low-Fructose Fruit

- 1 Cup Pitted Cranberries (frozen or fresh)
- 1/2 Cup Strawberries (frozen or fresh)
- 2 Cups Kale
- 4 Cups Spinach
- 1 Medium Lemon (peeled)
- 1/2 TSP Cinnamon
- 2 TBSP Garden in My Glass*
- 4 TBSP Clean Whey Protein**
- 1 TSP Hormone Healing Green Tea (optional)
- 2 TBSP Slimming Sugar Substitute (optional)***

DIRECTIONS

- Add all ingredients to a high-powered blender with 8 oz. cold water and a handful of ice.

- Blend for 2 minutes or until completely blended (i.e. no pieces of veggies or fruit are visible).

- Adjust the amount of water and ice for desired consistency and desired temperature.

TIP: Can't find some of these ingredients at your local grocery store? Have them delivered quickly and easily by visiting your SANE Superfoods Store at http://store.SANESolution.com.

NOTES

*You can add two additional serving of Non-Starchy Vegetables in place of the two tablespoons of Garden in My Glass. If you do not add more veggies and you do not add Garden in My Glass, track only two servings of Non-Starchy Vegetables per smoothie (instead of four servings).

**Only add protein if the smoothie is your entire meal. Vegetarians can use 6 TBSP of Clean Pea Protein (instead of Clean Whey Protein).

***To minimize sugar content, reduce fruit (other than lemon) and increase Slimming Sugar Substitute. If fruit is reduced by half or more, no Low-Fructose Fruit servings should be tracked. Due to their extremely low sugar content, lemons should not be reduced and do not need to be tracked.

CRANBERRY STRAWBERRY MAGIC

1 Serving   Prep: 1 min   Blend: 2 min   Total: 3 min

4 Non-Starchy Vegetables   1 Nutrient-Dense Protein   1 Low-Fructose Fruit

- 1 Cup Pitted Cranberries (frozen or fresh)
- 1/2 Cup Strawberries (frozen or fresh)
- 2 Cups Arugula
- 4 Cups Spinach
- 1 Medium Lemon (peeled)
- 1/2 TSP Cinnamon
- 2 TBSP Garden in My Glass*
- 4 TBSP Clean Whey Protein**
- 1 TSP Hormone Healing Green Tea (optional)
- 2 TBSP Slimming Sugar Substitute (optional)***

DIRECTIONS

- Add all ingredients to a high-powered blender with 8 oz. cold water and a handful of ice.

- Blend for 2 minutes or until completely blended (i.e. no pieces of veggies or fruit are visible).

- Adjust the amount of water and ice for desired consistency and desired temperature.

TIP: Can't find some of these ingredients at your local grocery store? Have them delivered quickly and easily by visiting your SANE Superfoods Store at http://store.SANESolution.com.

NOTES

*You can add two additional serving of Non-Starchy Vegetables in place of the two tablespoons of Garden in My Glass. If you do not add more veggies and you do not add Garden in My Glass, track only two servings of Non-Starchy Vegetables per smoothie (instead of four servings).

**Only add protein if the smoothie is your entire meal. Vegetarians can use 6 TBSP of Clean Pea Protein (instead of Clean Whey Protein).

***To minimize sugar content, reduce fruit (other than lemon) and increase Slimming Sugar Substitute. If fruit is reduced by half or more, no Low-Fructose Fruit servings should be tracked. Due to their extremely low sugar content, lemons should not be reduced and do not need to be tracked.

CRANBERRY SUNRISE

1 Serving　　Prep: 1 min　　Blend: 2 min　　Total: 3 min
4 Non-Starchy Vegetables　　1 Nutrient-Dense Protein　　1 Low-Fructose Fruit

- 1 1/2 Cups Pitted Cranberries (frozen or fresh)
- 6 Cups Romaine Lettuce
- 1 Medium Lemon (peeled)
- 1/2 TSP Cinnamon
- 2 TBSP Garden in My Glass*
- 4 TBSP Clean Whey Protein**
- 1 TSP Hormone Healing Green Tea (optional)
- 2 TBSP Slimming Sugar Substitute (optional)***

DIRECTIONS

- Add all ingredients to a high-powered blender with 8 oz. cold water and a handful of ice.

- Blend for 2 minutes or until completely blended (i.e. no pieces of veggies or fruit are visible).

- Adjust the amount of water and ice for desired consistency and desired temperature.

TIP: Can't find some of these ingredients at your local grocery store? Have them delivered quickly and easily by visiting your SANE Superfoods Store at http://store.SANESolution.com.

NOTES

*You can add two additional serving of Non-Starchy Vegetables in place of the two tablespoons of Garden in My Glass. If you do not add more veggies and you do not add Garden in My Glass, track only two servings of Non-Starchy Vegetables per smoothie (instead of four servings).

**Only add protein if the smoothie is your entire meal. Vegetarians can use 6 TBSP of Clean Pea Protein (instead of Clean Whey Protein).

***To minimize sugar content, reduce fruit (other than lemon) and increase Slimming Sugar Substitute. If fruit is reduced by half or more, no Low-Fructose Fruit servings should be tracked. Due to their extremely low sugar content, lemons should not be reduced and do not need to be tracked.

GRAPEFRUIT BLISS

1 Serving   Prep: 1 min   Blend: 2 min   Total: 3 min

4 Non-Starchy Vegetables   1 Nutrient-Dense Protein   1 Low-Fructose Fruit

- 1 Medium Grapefruit (peeled)
- 2 Cups Arugula
- 4 Cups Romaine Lettuce
- 1 Medium Lemon (peeled)
- 1/2 TSP Cinnamon
- 2 TBSP Garden in My Glass*
- 4 TBSP Clean Whey Protein**
- 1 TSP Hormone Healing Green Tea (optional)
- 2 TBSP Slimming Sugar Substitute (optional)***

DIRECTIONS

- Add all ingredients to a high-powered blender with 8 oz. cold water and a handful of ice.

- Blend for 2 minutes or until completely blended (i.e. no pieces of veggies or fruit are visible).

- Adjust the amount of water and ice for desired consistency and desired temperature.

TIP: Can't find some of these ingredients at your local grocery store? Have them delivered quickly and easily by visiting your SANE Superfoods Store at http://store.SANESolution.com.

NOTES

*You can add two additional serving of Non-Starchy Vegetables in place of the two tablespoons of Garden in My Glass. If you do not add more veggies and you do not add Garden in My Glass, track only two servings of Non-Starchy Vegetables per smoothie (instead of four servings).

**Only add protein if the smoothie is your entire meal. Vegetarians can use 6 TBSP of Clean Pea Protein (instead of Clean Whey Protein).

***To minimize sugar content, reduce fruit (other than lemon) and increase Slimming Sugar Substitute. If fruit is reduced by half or more, no Low-Fructose Fruit servings should be tracked. Due to their extremely low sugar content, lemons should not be reduced and do not need to be tracked.

GRAPEFRUIT GLEE

1 Serving   Prep: 1 min   Blend: 2 min   Total: 3 min
4 Non-Starchy Vegetables   1 Nutrient-Dense Protein   1 Low-Fructose Fruit

- 1 Medium Grapefruit (peeled)
- 2 Cups Chard
- 4 Cups Romaine Lettuce
- 1 Medium Lemon (peeled)
- 1/2 TSP Cinnamon
- 2 TBSP Garden in My Glass*
- 4 TBSP Clean Whey Protein**
- 1 TSP Hormone Healing Green Tea (optional)
- 2 TBSP Slimming Sugar Substitute (optional)***

DIRECTIONS

- Add all ingredients to a high-powered blender with 8 oz. cold water and a handful of ice.

- Blend for 2 minutes or until completely blended (i.e. no pieces of veggies or fruit are visible).

- Adjust the amount of water and ice for desired consistency and desired temperature.

TIP: Can't find some of these ingredients at your local grocery store? Have them delivered quickly and easily by visiting your SANE Superfoods Store at http://store.SANESolution.com.

NOTES

*You can add two additional serving of Non-Starchy Vegetables in place of the two tablespoons of Garden in My Glass. If you do not add more veggies and you do not add Garden in My Glass, track only two servings of Non-Starchy Vegetables per smoothie (instead of four servings).

**Only add protein if the smoothie is your entire meal. Vegetarians can use 6 TBSP of Clean Pea Protein (instead of Clean Whey Protein).

***To minimize sugar content, reduce fruit (other than lemon) and increase Slimming Sugar Substitute. If fruit is reduced by half or more, no Low-Fructose Fruit servings should be tracked. Due to their extremely low sugar content, lemons should not be reduced and do not need to be tracked.

MIXED BERRY BREEZE

1 Serving   Prep: 1 min   Blend: 2 min   Total: 3 min
4 Non-Starchy Vegetables   1 Nutrient-Dense Protein   1 Low-Fructose Fruit

- 1 Cup Mixed Berries (frozen or fresh)
- 2 Cups Kale
- 4 Cups Romaine Lettuce
- 1 Medium Lemon (peeled)
- 1/2 TSP Cinnamon
- 2 TBSP Garden in My Glass*
- 4 TBSP Clean Whey Protein**
- 1 TSP Hormone Healing Green Tea (optional)
- 2 TBSP Slimming Sugar Substitute (optional)***

DIRECTIONS

- Add all ingredients to a high-powered blender with 8 oz. cold water and a handful of ice.

- Blend for 2 minutes or until completely blended (i.e. no pieces of veggies or fruit are visible).

- Adjust the amount of water and ice for desired consistency and desired temperature.

TIP: Can't find some of these ingredients at your local grocery store? Have them delivered quickly and easily by visiting your SANE Superfoods Store at http://store.SANESolution.com.

NOTES

*You can add two additional serving of Non-Starchy Vegetables in place of the two tablespoons of Garden in My Glass. If you do not add more veggies and you do not add Garden in My Glass, track only two servings of Non-Starchy Vegetables per smoothie (instead of four servings).

**Only add protein if the smoothie is your entire meal. Vegetarians can use 6 TBSP of Clean Pea Protein (instead of Clean Whey Protein).

***To minimize sugar content, reduce fruit (other than lemon) and increase Slimming Sugar Substitute. If fruit is reduced by half or more, no Low-Fructose Fruit servings should be tracked. Due to their extremely low sugar content, lemons should not be reduced and do not need to be tracked.

MIXED BERRY WHIRL

1 Serving   Prep: 1 min   Blend: 2 min   Total: 3 min
4 Non-Starchy Vegetables   1 Nutrient-Dense Protein   1 Low-Fructose Fruit

- 1 Cup Mixed Berries (frozen or fresh)
- 3 Cups Spinach
- 3 Cups Romaine Lettuce
- 1 Medium Lemon (peeled)
- 1/2 TSP Cinnamon
- 2 TBSP Garden in My Glass*
- 4 TBSP Clean Whey Protein**
- 1 TSP Hormone Healing Green Tea (optional)
- 2 TBSP Slimming Sugar Substitute (optional)***

DIRECTIONS

- Add all ingredients to a high-powered blender with 8 oz. cold water and a handful of ice.

- Blend for 2 minutes or until completely blended (i.e. no pieces of veggies or fruit are visible).

- Adjust the amount of water and ice for desired consistency and desired temperature.

TIP: Can't find some of these ingredients at your local grocery store? Have them delivered quickly and easily by visiting your SANE Superfoods Store at http://store.SANESolution.com.

NOTES

*You can add two additional serving of Non-Starchy Vegetables in place of the two tablespoons of Garden in My Glass. If you do not add more veggies and you do not add Garden in My Glass, track only two servings of Non-Starchy Vegetables per smoothie (instead of four servings).

**Only add protein if the smoothie is your entire meal. Vegetarians can use 6 TBSP of Clean Pea Protein (instead of Clean Whey Protein).

***To minimize sugar content, reduce fruit (other than lemon) and increase Slimming Sugar Substitute. If fruit is reduced by half or more, no Low-Fructose Fruit servings should be tracked. Due to their extremely low sugar content, lemons should not be reduced and do not need to be tracked.

NECTARINE BLAST

1 Serving   Prep: 1 min   Blend: 2 min   Total: 3 min
4 Non-Starchy Vegetables   1 Nutrient-Dense Protein   1 Low-Fructose Fruit

- 1 Cup Nectarine Slices (frozen or fresh)
- 6 Cups Spinach
- 1 Medium Lemon (peeled)
- 1/2 TSP Cinnamon
- 2 TBSP Garden in My Glass*
- 4 TBSP Clean Whey Protein**
- 1 TSP Hormone Healing Green Tea (optional)
- 2 TBSP Slimming Sugar Substitute (optional)***

DIRECTIONS

- Add all ingredients to a high-powered blender with 8 oz. cold water and a handful of ice.

- Blend for 2 minutes or until completely blended (i.e. no pieces of veggies or fruit are visible).

- Adjust the amount of water and ice for desired consistency and desired temperature.

TIP: Can't find some of these ingredients at your local grocery store? Have them delivered quickly and easily by visiting your SANE Superfoods Store at http://store.SANESolution.com.

NOTES

*You can add two additional serving of Non-Starchy Vegetables in place of the two tablespoons of Garden in My Glass. If you do not add more veggies and you do not add Garden in My Glass, track only two servings of Non-Starchy Vegetables per smoothie (instead of four servings).

**Only add protein if the smoothie is your entire meal. Vegetarians can use 6 TBSP of Clean Pea Protein (instead of Clean Whey Protein).

***To minimize sugar content, reduce fruit (other than lemon) and increase Slimming Sugar Substitute. If fruit is reduced by half or more, no Low-Fructose Fruit servings should be tracked. Due to their extremely low sugar content, lemons should not be reduced and do not need to be tracked.

NECTARINE BLISS

1 Serving   Prep: 1 min   Blend: 2 min   Total: 3 min
4 Non-Starchy Vegetables   1 Nutrient-Dense Protein   1 Low-Fructose Fruit

- 1 Cup Nectarine Slices (frozen or fresh)
- 2 Cups Arugula
- 4 Cups Romaine Lettuce
- 1 Medium Lemon (peeled)
- 1/2 TSP Cinnamon
- 2 TBSP Garden in My Glass*
- 4 TBSP Clean Whey Protein**
- 1 TSP Hormone Healing Green Tea (optional)
- 2 TBSP Slimming Sugar Substitute (optional)***

DIRECTIONS

- Add all ingredients to a high-powered blender with 8 oz. cold water and a handful of ice.

- Blend for 2 minutes or until completely blended (i.e. no pieces of veggies or fruit are visible).

- Adjust the amount of water and ice for desired consistency and desired temperature.

TIP: Can't find some of these ingredients at your local grocery store? Have them delivered quickly and easily by visiting your SANE Superfoods Store at http://store.SANESolution.com.

NOTES

*You can add two additional serving of Non-Starchy Vegetables in place of the two tablespoons of Garden in My Glass. If you do not add more veggies and you do not add Garden in My Glass, track only two servings of Non-Starchy Vegetables per smoothie (instead of four servings).

**Only add protein if the smoothie is your entire meal. Vegetarians can use 6 TBSP of Clean Pea Protein (instead of Clean Whey Protein).

***To minimize sugar content, reduce fruit (other than lemon) and increase Slimming Sugar Substitute. If fruit is reduced by half or more, no Low-Fructose Fruit servings should be tracked. Due to their extremely low sugar content, lemons should not be reduced and do not need to be tracked.

NECTARINE BREEZE

1 Serving   Prep: 1 min   Blend: 2 min   Total: 3 min
4 Non-Starchy Vegetables   1 Nutrient-Dense Protein   1 Low-Fructose Fruit

- 1 Cup Nectarine Slices (frozen or fresh)
- 2 Cups Kale
- 4 Cups Romaine Lettuce
- 1 Medium Lemon (peeled)
- 1/2 TSP Cinnamon
- 2 TBSP Garden in My Glass*
- 4 TBSP Clean Whey Protein**
- 1 TSP Hormone Healing Green Tea (optional)
- 2 TBSP Slimming Sugar Substitute (optional)***

DIRECTIONS

- Add all ingredients to a high-powered blender with 8 oz. cold water and a handful of ice.

- Blend for 2 minutes or until completely blended (i.e. no pieces of veggies or fruit are visible).

- Adjust the amount of water and ice for desired consistency and desired temperature.

TIP: Can't find some of these ingredients at your local grocery store? Have them delivered quickly and easily by visiting your SANE Superfoods Store at http://store.SANESolution.com.

NOTES

*You can add two additional serving of Non-Starchy Vegetables in place of the two tablespoons of Garden in My Glass. If you do not add more veggies and you do not add Garden in My Glass, track only two servings of Non-Starchy Vegetables per smoothie (instead of four servings).

**Only add protein if the smoothie is your entire meal. Vegetarians can use 6 TBSP of Clean Pea Protein (instead of Clean Whey Protein).

***To minimize sugar content, reduce fruit (other than lemon) and increase Slimming Sugar Substitute. If fruit is reduced by half or more, no Low-Fructose Fruit servings should be tracked. Due to their extremely low sugar content, lemons should not be reduced and do not need to be tracked.

NECTARINE CRANBERRY BLAST

1 Serving   Prep: 1 min   Blend: 2 min   Total: 3 min
4 Non-Starchy Vegetables   1 Nutrient-Dense Protein   1 Low-Fructose Fruit

- 1/2 Cup Nectarine Slices (frozen or fresh)
- 1 Cup Pitted Cranberries (frozen or fresh)
- 6 Cups Spinach
- 1 Medium Lemon (peeled)
- 1/2 TSP Cinnamon
- 2 TBSP Garden in My Glass*
- 4 TBSP Clean Whey Protein**
- 1 TSP Hormone Healing Green Tea (optional)
- 2 TBSP Slimming Sugar Substitute (optional)***

DIRECTIONS

- Add all ingredients to a high-powered blender with 8 oz. cold water and a handful of ice.

- Blend for 2 minutes or until completely blended (i.e. no pieces of veggies or fruit are visible).

- Adjust the amount of water and ice for desired consistency and desired temperature.

TIP: Can't find some of these ingredients at your local grocery store? Have them delivered quickly and easily by visiting your SANE Superfoods Store at http://store.SANESolution.com.

NOTES

*You can add two additional serving of Non-Starchy Vegetables in place of the two tablespoons of Garden in My Glass. If you do not add more veggies and you do not add Garden in My Glass, track only two servings of Non-Starchy Vegetables per smoothie (instead of four servings).

**Only add protein if the smoothie is your entire meal. Vegetarians can use 6 TBSP of Clean Pea Protein (instead of Clean Whey Protein).

***To minimize sugar content, reduce fruit (other than lemon) and increase Slimming Sugar Substitute. If fruit is reduced by half or more, no Low-Fructose Fruit servings should be tracked. Due to their extremely low sugar content, lemons should not be reduced and do not need to be tracked.

NECTARINE CRANBERRY BLISS

1 Serving   Prep: 1 min   Blend: 2 min   Total: 3 min
4 Non-Starchy Vegetables   1 Nutrient-Dense Protein   1 Low-Fructose Fruit

- 1/2 Cup Nectarine Slices (frozen or fresh)
- 1 Cup Pitted Cranberries (frozen or fresh)
- 2 Cups Arugula
- 4 Cups Romaine Lettuce
- 1 Medium Lemon (peeled)
- 1/2 TSP Cinnamon
- 2 TBSP Garden in My Glass*
- 4 TBSP Clean Whey Protein**
- 1 TSP Hormone Healing Green Tea (optional)
- 2 TBSP Slimming Sugar Substitute (optional)***

DIRECTIONS

- Add all ingredients to a high-powered blender with 8 oz. cold water and a handful of ice.

- Blend for 2 minutes or until completely blended (i.e. no pieces of veggies or fruit are visible).

- Adjust the amount of water and ice for desired consistency and desired temperature.

TIP: Can't find some of these ingredients at your local grocery store? Have them delivered quickly and easily by visiting your SANE Superfoods Store at http://store.SANESolution.com.

NOTES

*You can add two additional serving of Non-Starchy Vegetables in place of the two tablespoons of Garden in My Glass. If you do not add more veggies and you do not add Garden in My Glass, track only two servings of Non-Starchy Vegetables per smoothie (instead of four servings).

**Only add protein if the smoothie is your entire meal. Vegetarians can use 6 TBSP of Clean Pea Protein (instead of Clean Whey Protein).

***To minimize sugar content, reduce fruit (other than lemon) and increase Slimming Sugar Substitute. If fruit is reduced by half or more, no Low-Fructose Fruit servings should be tracked. Due to their extremely low sugar content, lemons should not be reduced and do not need to be tracked.

NECTARINE CRANBERRY ESCAPE

1 Serving   Prep: 1 min   Blend: 2 min   Total: 3 min
4 Non-Starchy Vegetables   1 Nutrient-Dense Protein   1 Low-Fructose Fruit

- 1/2 Cup Nectarine Slices (frozen or fresh)
- 1 Cup Pitted Cranberries (frozen or fresh)
- 2 Cups Chard
- 4 Cups Spinach
- 1 Medium Lemon (peeled)
- 1/2 TSP Cinnamon
- 2 TBSP Garden in My Glass*
- 4 TBSP Clean Whey Protein**
- 1 TSP Hormone Healing Green Tea (optional)
- 2 TBSP Slimming Sugar Substitute (optional)***

DIRECTIONS

- Add all ingredients to a high-powered blender with 8 oz. cold water and a handful of ice.

- Blend for 2 minutes or until completely blended (i.e. no pieces of veggies or fruit are visible).

- Adjust the amount of water and ice for desired consistency and desired temperature.

TIP: Can't find some of these ingredients at your local grocery store? Have them delivered quickly and easily by visiting your SANE Superfoods Store at http://store.SANESolution.com.

NOTES

*You can add two additional serving of Non-Starchy Vegetables in place of the two tablespoons of Garden in My Glass. If you do not add more veggies and you do not add Garden in My Glass, track only two servings of Non-Starchy Vegetables per smoothie (instead of four servings).

**Only add protein if the smoothie is your entire meal. Vegetarians can use 6 TBSP of Clean Pea Protein (instead of Clean Whey Protein).

***To minimize sugar content, reduce fruit (other than lemon) and increase Slimming Sugar Substitute. If fruit is reduced by half or more, no Low-Fructose Fruit servings should be tracked. Due to their extremely low sugar content, lemons should not be reduced and do not need to be tracked.

NECTARINE DELIGHT

1 Serving   Prep: 1 min   Blend: 2 min   Total: 3 min
4 Non-Starchy Vegetables   1 Nutrient-Dense Protein   1 Low-Fructose Fruit

- 1 Cup Nectarine Slices (frozen or fresh)
- 2 Cups Kale
- 4 Cups Spinach
- 1 Medium Lemon (peeled)
- 1/2 TSP Cinnamon
- 2 TBSP Garden in My Glass*
- 4 TBSP Clean Whey Protein**
- 1 TSP Hormone Healing Green Tea (optional)
- 2 TBSP Slimming Sugar Substitute (optional)***

DIRECTIONS

- Add all ingredients to a high-powered blender with 8 oz. cold water and a handful of ice.

- Blend for 2 minutes or until completely blended (i.e. no pieces of veggies or fruit are visible).

- Adjust the amount of water and ice for desired consistency and desired temperature.

TIP: Can't find some of these ingredients at your local grocery store? Have them delivered quickly and easily by visiting your SANE Superfoods Store at http://store.SANESolution.com.

NOTES

*You can add two additional serving of Non-Starchy Vegetables in place of the two tablespoons of Garden in My Glass. If you do not add more veggies and you do not add Garden in My Glass, track only two servings of Non-Starchy Vegetables per smoothie (instead of four servings).

**Only add protein if the smoothie is your entire meal. Vegetarians can use 6 TBSP of Clean Pea Protein (instead of Clean Whey Protein).

***To minimize sugar content, reduce fruit (other than lemon) and increase Slimming Sugar Substitute. If fruit is reduced by half or more, no Low-Fructose Fruit servings should be tracked. Due to their extremely low sugar content, lemons should not be reduced and do not need to be tracked.

NECTARINE DREAM

1 Serving   Prep: 1 min   Blend: 2 min   Total: 3 min
4 Non-Starchy Vegetables   1 Nutrient-Dense Protein   1 Low-Fructose Fruit

- 1 Cup Nectarine Slices (frozen or fresh)
- 3 Cups Mixed Greens
- 3 Cups Spinach
- 1 Medium Lemon (peeled)
- 1/2 TSP Cinnamon
- 2 TBSP Garden in My Glass*
- 4 TBSP Clean Whey Protein**
- 1 TSP Hormone Healing Green Tea (optional)
- 2 TBSP Slimming Sugar Substitute (optional)***

DIRECTIONS

- Add all ingredients to a high-powered blender with 8 oz. cold water and a handful of ice.

- Blend for 2 minutes or until completely blended (i.e. no pieces of veggies or fruit are visible).

- Adjust the amount of water and ice for desired consistency and desired temperature.

TIP: Can't find some of these ingredients at your local grocery store? Have them delivered quickly and easily by visiting your SANE Superfoods Store at http://store.SANESolution.com.

NOTES

*You can add two additional serving of Non-Starchy Vegetables in place of the two tablespoons of Garden in My Glass. If you do not add more veggies and you do not add Garden in My Glass, track only two servings of Non-Starchy Vegetables per smoothie (instead of four servings).

**Only add protein if the smoothie is your entire meal. Vegetarians can use 6 TBSP of Clean Pea Protein (instead of Clean Whey Protein).

***To minimize sugar content, reduce fruit (other than lemon) and increase Slimming Sugar Substitute. If fruit is reduced by half or more, no Low-Fructose Fruit servings should be tracked. Due to their extremely low sugar content, lemons should not be reduced and do not need to be tracked.

NECTARINE ESCAPE

1 Serving   Prep: 1 min   Blend: 2 min   Total: 3 min
4 Non-Starchy Vegetables   1 Nutrient-Dense Protein   1 Low-Fructose Fruit

- 1 Cup Nectarine Slices (frozen or fresh)
- 2 Cups Chard
- 4 Cups Spinach
- 1 Medium Lemon (peeled)
- 1/2 TSP Cinnamon
- 2 TBSP Garden in My Glass*
- 4 TBSP Clean Whey Protein**
- 1 TSP Hormone Healing Green Tea (optional)
- 2 TBSP Slimming Sugar Substitute (optional)***

DIRECTIONS

- Add all ingredients to a high-powered blender with 8 oz. cold water and a handful of ice.

- Blend for 2 minutes or until completely blended (i.e. no pieces of veggies or fruit are visible).

- Adjust the amount of water and ice for desired consistency and desired temperature.

TIP: Can't find some of these ingredients at your local grocery store? Have them delivered quickly and easily by visiting your SANE Superfoods Store at http://store.SANESolution.com.

NOTES

*You can add two additional serving of Non-Starchy Vegetables in place of the two tablespoons of Garden in My Glass. If you do not add more veggies and you do not add Garden in My Glass, track only two servings of Non-Starchy Vegetables per smoothie (instead of four servings).

**Only add protein if the smoothie is your entire meal. Vegetarians can use 6 TBSP of Clean Pea Protein (instead of Clean Whey Protein).

***To minimize sugar content, reduce fruit (other than lemon) and increase Slimming Sugar Substitute. If fruit is reduced by half or more, no Low-Fructose Fruit servings should be tracked. Due to their extremely low sugar content, lemons should not be reduced and do not need to be tracked.

NECTARINE SUNRISE

1 Serving   Prep: 1 min   Blend: 2 min   Total: 3 min
4 Non-Starchy Vegetables   1 Nutrient-Dense Protein   1 Low-Fructose Fruit

- 1 Cup Nectarine Slices (frozen or fresh)
- 6 Cups Romaine Lettuce
- 1 Medium Lemon (peeled)
- 1/2 TSP Cinnamon
- 2 TBSP Garden in My Glass*
- 4 TBSP Clean Whey Protein**
- 1 TSP Hormone Healing Green Tea (optional)
- 2 TBSP Slimming Sugar Substitute (optional)***

DIRECTIONS

- Add all ingredients to a high-powered blender with 8 oz. cold water and a handful of ice.

- Blend for 2 minutes or until completely blended (i.e. no pieces of veggies or fruit are visible).

- Adjust the amount of water and ice for desired consistency and desired temperature.

TIP: Can't find some of these ingredients at your local grocery store? Have them delivered quickly and easily by visiting your SANE Superfoods Store at http://store.SANESolution.com.

NOTES

*You can add two additional serving of Non-Starchy Vegetables in place of the two tablespoons of Garden in My Glass. If you do not add more veggies and you do not add Garden in My Glass, track only two servings of Non-Starchy Vegetables per smoothie (instead of four servings).

**Only add protein if the smoothie is your entire meal. Vegetarians can use 6 TBSP of Clean Pea Protein (instead of Clean Whey Protein).

***To minimize sugar content, reduce fruit (other than lemon) and increase Slimming Sugar Substitute. If fruit is reduced by half or more, no Low-Fructose Fruit servings should be tracked. Due to their extremely low sugar content, lemons should not be reduced and do not need to be tracked.

ORANGE DREAM

1 Serving   Prep: 1 min   Blend: 2 min   Total: 3 min
4 Non-Starchy Vegetables   1 Nutrient-Dense Protein   1 Low-Fructose Fruit

- 1 Medium Orange (peeled)
- 3 Cups Mixed Greens
- 3 Cups Spinach
- 1 Medium Lemon (peeled)
- 1/2 TSP Cinnamon
- 2 TBSP Garden in My Glass*
- 4 TBSP Clean Whey Protein**
- 1 TSP Hormone Healing Green Tea (optional)
- 2 TBSP Slimming Sugar Substitute (optional)***

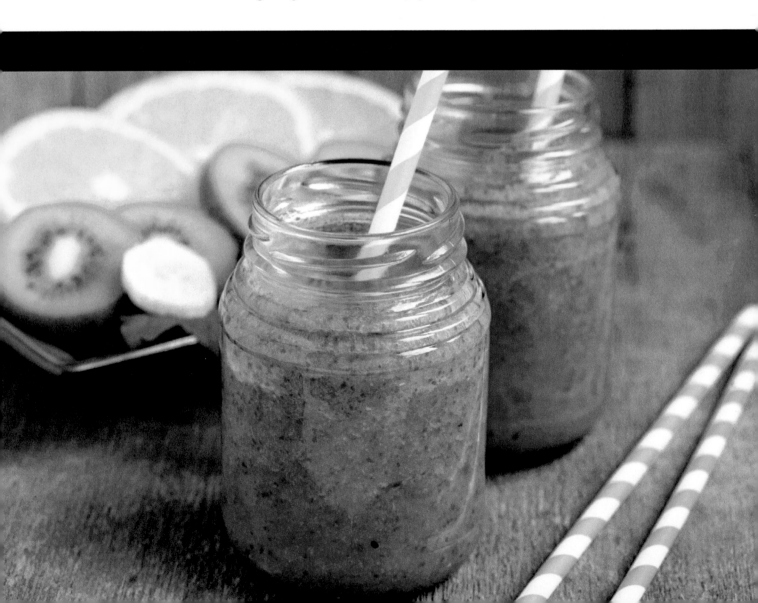

DIRECTIONS

- Add all ingredients to a high-powered blender with 8 oz. cold water and a handful of ice.

- Blend for 2 minutes or until completely blended (i.e. no pieces of veggies or fruit are visible).

- Adjust the amount of water and ice for desired consistency and desired temperature.

TIP: Can't find some of these ingredients at your local grocery store? Have them delivered quickly and easily by visiting your SANE Superfoods Store at http://store.SANESolution.com.

NOTES

*You can add two additional serving of Non-Starchy Vegetables in place of the two tablespoons of Garden in My Glass. If you do not add more veggies and you do not add Garden in My Glass, track only two servings of Non-Starchy Vegetables per smoothie (instead of four servings).

**Only add protein if the smoothie is your entire meal. Vegetarians can use 6 TBSP of Clean Pea Protein (instead of Clean Whey Protein).

***To minimize sugar content, reduce fruit (other than lemon) and increase Slimming Sugar Substitute. If fruit is reduced by half or more, no Low-Fructose Fruit servings should be tracked. Due to their extremely low sugar content, lemons should not be reduced and do not need to be tracked.

ORANGE SUNRISE

1 Serving   Prep: 1 min   Blend: 2 min   Total: 3 min
4 Non-Starchy Vegetables   1 Nutrient-Dense Protein   1 Low-Fructose Fruit

- 1 Medium Orange (peeled)
- 6 Cups Romaine Lettuce
- 1 Medium Lemon (peeled)
- 1/2 TSP Cinnamon
- 2 TBSP Garden in My Glass*
- 4 TBSP Clean Whey Protein**
- 1 TSP Hormone Healing Green Tea (optional)
- 2 TBSP Slimming Sugar Substitute (optional)***

DIRECTIONS

- Add all ingredients to a high-powered blender with 8 oz. cold water and a handful of ice.

- Blend for 2 minutes or until completely blended (i.e. no pieces of veggies or fruit are visible).

- Adjust the amount of water and ice for desired consistency and desired temperature.

TIP: Can't find some of these ingredients at your local grocery store? Have them delivered quickly and easily by visiting your SANE Superfoods Store at http://store.SANESolution.com.

NOTES

*You can add two additional serving of Non-Starchy Vegetables in place of the two tablespoons of Garden in My Glass. If you do not add more veggies and you do not add Garden in My Glass, track only two servings of Non-Starchy Vegetables per smoothie (instead of four servings).

**Only add protein if the smoothie is your entire meal. Vegetarians can use 6 TBSP of Clean Pea Protein (instead of Clean Whey Protein).

***To minimize sugar content, reduce fruit (other than lemon) and increase Slimming Sugar Substitute. If fruit is reduced by half or more, no Low-Fructose Fruit servings should be tracked. Due to their extremely low sugar content, lemons should not be reduced and do not need to be tracked.

ORANGE WHIRL

1 Serving   Prep: 1 min   Blend: 2 min   Total: 3 min
4 Non-Starchy Vegetables   1 Nutrient-Dense Protein   1 Low-Fructose Fruit

- 1 Medium Orange (peeled)
- 3 Cups Spinach
- 3 Cups Romaine Lettuce
- 1 Medium Lemon (peeled)
- 1/2 TSP Cinnamon
- 2 TBSP Garden in My Glass*
- 4 TBSP Clean Whey Protein**
- 1 TSP Hormone Healing Green Tea (optional)
- 2 TBSP Slimming Sugar Substitute (optional)***

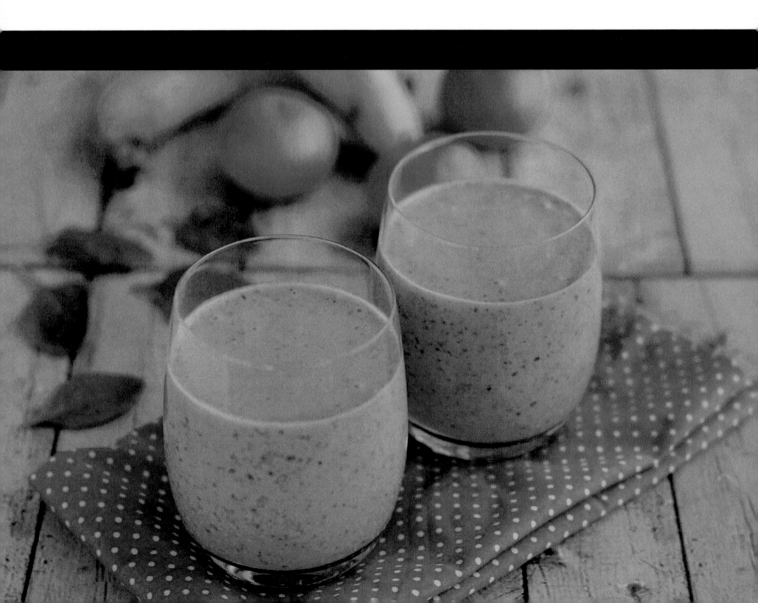

DIRECTIONS

- Add all ingredients to a high-powered blender with 8 oz. cold water and a handful of ice.

- Blend for 2 minutes or until completely blended (i.e. no pieces of veggies or fruit are visible).

- Adjust the amount of water and ice for desired consistency and desired temperature.

TIP: Can't find some of these ingredients at your local grocery store? Have them delivered quickly and easily by visiting your SANE Superfoods Store at http://store.SANESolution.com.

NOTES

*You can add two additional serving of Non-Starchy Vegetables in place of the two tablespoons of Garden in My Glass. If you do not add more veggies and you do not add Garden in My Glass, track only two servings of Non-Starchy Vegetables per smoothie (instead of four servings).

**Only add protein if the smoothie is your entire meal. Vegetarians can use 6 TBSP of Clean Pea Protein (instead of Clean Whey Protein).

***To minimize sugar content, reduce fruit (other than lemon) and increase Slimming Sugar Substitute. If fruit is reduced by half or more, no Low-Fructose Fruit servings should be tracked. Due to their extremely low sugar content, lemons should not be reduced and do not need to be tracked.

PEACH BLAST

1 Serving   Prep: 1 min   Blend: 2 min   Total: 3 min

4 Non-Starchy Vegetables   1 Nutrient-Dense Protein   1 Low-Fructose Fruit

- 1 Cup Peach Slices (frozen or fresh)
- 6 Cups Spinach
- 1 Medium Lemon (peeled)
- 1/2 TSP Cinnamon
- 2 TBSP Garden in My Glass*
- 4 TBSP Clean Whey Protein**
- 1 TSP Hormone Healing Green Tea (optional)
- 2 TBSP Slimming Sugar Substitute (optional)***

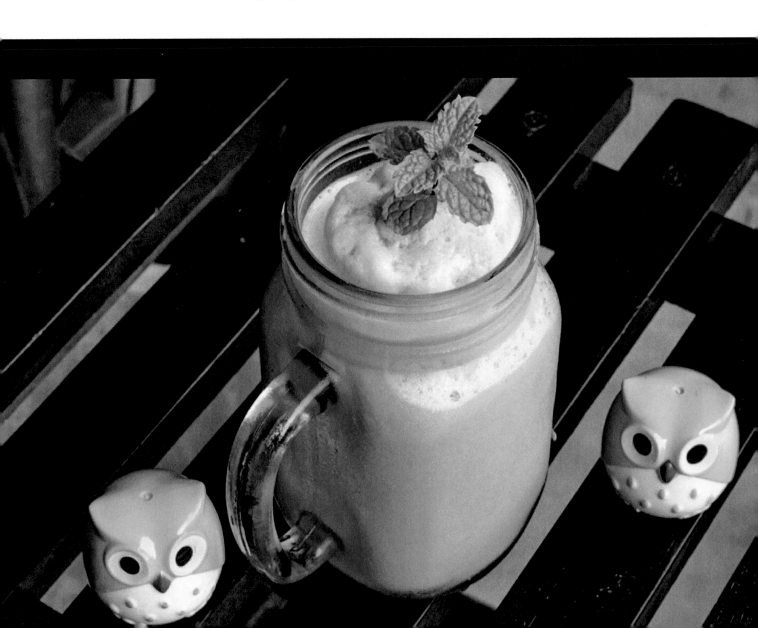

DIRECTIONS

- Add all ingredients to a high-powered blender with 8 oz. cold water and a handful of ice.

- Blend for 2 minutes or until completely blended (i.e. no pieces of veggies or fruit are visible).

- Adjust the amount of water and ice for desired consistency and desired temperature.

TIP: Can't find some of these ingredients at your local grocery store? Have them delivered quickly and easily by visiting your SANE Superfoods Store at http://store.SANESolution.com.

NOTES

*You can add two additional serving of Non-Starchy Vegetables in place of the two tablespoons of Garden in My Glass. If you do not add more veggies and you do not add Garden in My Glass, track only two servings of Non-Starchy Vegetables per smoothie (instead of four servings).

**Only add protein if the smoothie is your entire meal. Vegetarians can use 6 TBSP of Clean Pea Protein (instead of Clean Whey Protein).

***To minimize sugar content, reduce fruit (other than lemon) and increase Slimming Sugar Substitute. If fruit is reduced by half or more, no Low-Fructose Fruit servings should be tracked. Due to their extremely low sugar content, lemons should not be reduced and do not need to be tracked.

PEACH DELIGHT

1 Serving   Prep: 1 min   Blend: 2 min   Total: 3 min
4 Non-Starchy Vegetables   1 Nutrient-Dense Protein   1 Low-Fructose Fruit

- 1 Cup Peach Slices (frozen or fresh)
- 2 Cups Kale
- 4 Cups Spinach
- 1 Medium Lemon (peeled)
- 1/2 TSP Cinnamon
- 2 TBSP Garden in My Glass*
- 4 TBSP Clean Whey Protein**
- 1 TSP Hormone Healing Green Tea (optional)
- 2 TBSP Slimming Sugar Substitute (optional)***

DIRECTIONS

- Add all ingredients to a high-powered blender with 8 oz. cold water and a handful of ice.

- Blend for 2 minutes or until completely blended (i.e. no pieces of veggies or fruit are visible).

- Adjust the amount of water and ice for desired consistency and desired temperature.

TIP: Can't find some of these ingredients at your local grocery store? Have them delivered quickly and easily by visiting your SANE Superfoods Store at http://store.SANESolution.com.

NOTES

*You can add two additional serving of Non-Starchy Vegetables in place of the two tablespoons of Garden in My Glass. If you do not add more veggies and you do not add Garden in My Glass, track only two servings of Non-Starchy Vegetables per smoothie (instead of four servings).

**Only add protein if the smoothie is your entire meal. Vegetarians can use 6 TBSP of Clean Pea Protein (instead of Clean Whey Protein).

***To minimize sugar content, reduce fruit (other than lemon) and increase Slimming Sugar Substitute. If fruit is reduced by half or more, no Low-Fructose Fruit servings should be tracked. Due to their extremely low sugar content, lemons should not be reduced and do not need to be tracked.

PEACH ESCAPE

1 Serving   Prep: 1 min   Blend: 2 min   Total: 3 min
4 Non-Starchy Vegetables   1 Nutrient-Dense Protein   1 Low-Fructose Fruit

- 1 Cup Peach Slices (frozen or fresh)
- 2 Cups Chard
- 4 Cups Spinach
- 1 Medium Lemon (peeled)
- 1/2 TSP Cinnamon
- 2 TBSP Garden in My Glass*
- 4 TBSP Clean Whey Protein**
- 1 TSP Hormone Healing Green Tea (optional)
- 2 TBSP Slimming Sugar Substitute (optional)***

DIRECTIONS

- Add all ingredients to a high-powered blender with 8 oz. cold water and a handful of ice.

- Blend for 2 minutes or until completely blended (i.e. no pieces of veggies or fruit are visible).

- Adjust the amount of water and ice for desired consistency and desired temperature.

TIP: Can't find some of these ingredients at your local grocery store? Have them delivered quickly and easily by visiting your SANE Superfoods Store at http://store.SANESolution.com.

NOTES

*You can add two additional serving of Non-Starchy Vegetables in place of the two tablespoons of Garden in My Glass. If you do not add more veggies and you do not add Garden in My Glass, track only two servings of Non-Starchy Vegetables per smoothie (instead of four servings).

**Only add protein if the smoothie is your entire meal. Vegetarians can use 6 TBSP of Clean Pea Protein (instead of Clean Whey Protein).

***To minimize sugar content, reduce fruit (other than lemon) and increase Slimming Sugar Substitute. If fruit is reduced by half or more, no Low-Fructose Fruit servings should be tracked. Due to their extremely low sugar content, lemons should not be reduced and do not need to be tracked.

PEACH GRAPEFRUIT DELIGHT

1 Serving   Prep: 1 min   Blend: 2 min   Total: 3 min
4 Non-Starchy Vegetables   1 Nutrient-Dense Protein   1 Low-Fructose Fruit

- 1/2 Cup Peach Slices (frozen or fresh)
- 1/2 Medium Grapefruit (peeled)
- 2 Cups Kale
- 4 Cups Spinach
- 1 Medium Lemon (peeled)
- 1/2 TSP Cinnamon
- 2 TBSP Garden in My Glass*
- 4 TBSP Clean Whey Protein**
- 1 TSP Hormone Healing Green Tea (optional)
- 2 TBSP Slimming Sugar Substitute (optional)***

DIRECTIONS

- Add all ingredients to a high-powered blender with 8 oz. cold water and a handful of ice.

- Blend for 2 minutes or until completely blended (i.e. no pieces of veggies or fruit are visible).

- Adjust the amount of water and ice for desired consistency and desired temperature.

TIP: Can't find some of these ingredients at your local grocery store? Have them delivered quickly and easily by visiting your SANE Superfoods Store at http://store.SANESolution.com.

NOTES

*You can add two additional serving of Non-Starchy Vegetables in place of the two tablespoons of Garden in My Glass. If you do not add more veggies and you do not add Garden in My Glass, track only two servings of Non-Starchy Vegetables per smoothie (instead of four servings).

**Only add protein if the smoothie is your entire meal. Vegetarians can use 6 TBSP of Clean Pea Protein (instead of Clean Whey Protein).

***To minimize sugar content, reduce fruit (other than lemon) and increase Slimming Sugar Substitute. If fruit is reduced by half or more, no Low-Fructose Fruit servings should be tracked. Due to their extremely low sugar content, lemons should not be reduced and do not need to be tracked.

PEACH GRAPEFRUIT GLEE

1 Serving   Prep: 1 min   Blend: 2 min   Total: 3 min
4 Non-Starchy Vegetables   1 Nutrient-Dense Protein   1 Low-Fructose Fruit

- 1/2 Cup Peach Slices (frozen or fresh)
- 1/2 Medium Grapefruit (peeled)
- 2 Cups Chard
- 4 Cups Romaine Lettuce
- 1 Medium Lemon (peeled)
- 1/2 TSP Cinnamon
- 2 TBSP Garden in My Glass*
- 4 TBSP Clean Whey Protein**
- 1 TSP Hormone Healing Green Tea (optional)
- 2 TBSP Slimming Sugar Substitute (optional)***

DIRECTIONS

- Add all ingredients to a high-powered blender with 8 oz. cold water and a handful of ice.

- Blend for 2 minutes or until completely blended (i.e. no pieces of veggies or fruit are visible).

- Adjust the amount of water and ice for desired consistency and desired temperature.

TIP: Can't find some of these ingredients at your local grocery store? Have them delivered quickly and easily by visiting your SANE Superfoods Store at http://store.SANESolution.com.

NOTES

*You can add two additional serving of Non-Starchy Vegetables in place of the two tablespoons of Garden in My Glass. If you do not add more veggies and you do not add Garden in My Glass, track only two servings of Non-Starchy Vegetables per smoothie (instead of four servings).

**Only add protein if the smoothie is your entire meal. Vegetarians can use 6 TBSP of Clean Pea Protein (instead of Clean Whey Protein).

***To minimize sugar content, reduce fruit (other than lemon) and increase Slimming Sugar Substitute. If fruit is reduced by half or more, no Low-Fructose Fruit servings should be tracked. Due to their extremely low sugar content, lemons should not be reduced and do not need to be tracked.

PEACH GRAPEFRUIT MAGIC

1 Serving   Prep: 1 min   Blend: 2 min   Total: 3 min
4 Non-Starchy Vegetables   1 Nutrient-Dense Protein   1 Low-Fructose Fruit

- 1/2 Cup Peach Slices (frozen or fresh)
- 1/2 Medium Grapefruit (peeled)
- 2 Cups Arugula
- 4 Cups Spinach
- 1 Medium Lemon (peeled)
- 1/2 TSP Cinnamon
- 2 TBSP Garden in My Glass*
- 4 TBSP Clean Whey Protein**
- 1 TSP Hormone Healing Green Tea (optional)
- 2 TBSP Slimming Sugar Substitute (optional)***

DIRECTIONS

- Add all ingredients to a high-powered blender with 8 oz. cold water and a handful of ice.

- Blend for 2 minutes or until completely blended (i.e. no pieces of veggies or fruit are visible).

- Adjust the amount of water and ice for desired consistency and desired temperature.

TIP: Can't find some of these ingredients at your local grocery store? Have them delivered quickly and easily by visiting your SANE Superfoods Store at http://store.SANESolution.com.

NOTES

*You can add two additional serving of Non-Starchy Vegetables in place of the two tablespoons of Garden in My Glass. If you do not add more veggies and you do not add Garden in My Glass, track only two servings of Non-Starchy Vegetables per smoothie (instead of four servings).

**Only add protein if the smoothie is your entire meal. Vegetarians can use 6 TBSP of Clean Pea Protein (instead of Clean Whey Protein).

***To minimize sugar content, reduce fruit (other than lemon) and increase Slimming Sugar Substitute. If fruit is reduced by half or more, no Low-Fructose Fruit servings should be tracked. Due to their extremely low sugar content, lemons should not be reduced and do not need to be tracked.

PEACH GRAPEFRUIT WHIRL

1 Serving   Prep: 1 min   Blend: 2 min   Total: 3 min

4 Non-Starchy Vegetables   1 Nutrient-Dense Protein   1 Low-Fructose Fruit

- 1/2 Cup Peach Slices (frozen or fresh)
- 1/2 Medium Grapefruit (peeled)
- 3 Cups Spinach
- 3 Cups Romaine Lettuce
- 1 Medium Lemon (peeled)
- 1/2 TSP Cinnamon
- 2 TBSP Garden in My Glass*
- 4 TBSP Clean Whey Protein**
- 1 TSP Hormone Healing Green Tea (optional)
- 2 TBSP Slimming Sugar Substitute (optional)***

DIRECTIONS

- Add all ingredients to a high-powered blender with 8 oz. cold water and a handful of ice.

- Blend for 2 minutes or until completely blended (i.e. no pieces of veggies or fruit are visible).

- Adjust the amount of water and ice for desired consistency and desired temperature.

TIP: Can't find some of these ingredients at your local grocery store? Have them delivered quickly and easily by visiting your SANE Superfoods Store at http://store.SANESolution.com.

NOTES

*You can add two additional serving of Non-Starchy Vegetables in place of the two tablespoons of Garden in My Glass. If you do not add more veggies and you do not add Garden in My Glass, track only two servings of Non-Starchy Vegetables per smoothie (instead of four servings).

**Only add protein if the smoothie is your entire meal. Vegetarians can use 6 TBSP of Clean Pea Protein (instead of Clean Whey Protein).

***To minimize sugar content, reduce fruit (other than lemon) and increase Slimming Sugar Substitute. If fruit is reduced by half or more, no Low-Fructose Fruit servings should be tracked. Due to their extremely low sugar content, lemons should not be reduced and do not need to be tracked.

PEACH NECTARINE DELIGHT

1 Serving   Prep: 1 min   Blend: 2 min   Total: 3 min
4 Non-Starchy Vegetables   1 Nutrient-Dense Protein   1 Low-Fructose Fruit

- 1/2 Cup Peach Slices (frozen or fresh)
- 1/2 Cup Nectarine Slices (frozen or fresh)
- 2 Cups Kale
- 4 Cups Spinach
- 1 Medium Lemon (peeled)
- 1/2 TSP Cinnamon
- 2 TBSP Garden in My Glass*
- 4 TBSP Clean Whey Protein**
- 1 TSP Hormone Healing Green Tea (optional)
- 2 TBSP Slimming Sugar Substitute (optional)***

DIRECTIONS

- Add all ingredients to a high-powered blender with 8 oz. cold water and a handful of ice.

- Blend for 2 minutes or until completely blended (i.e. no pieces of veggies or fruit are visible).

- Adjust the amount of water and ice for desired consistency and desired temperature.

TIP: Can't find some of these ingredients at your local grocery store? Have them delivered quickly and easily by visiting your SANE Superfoods Store at http://store.SANESolution.com.

NOTES

*You can add two additional serving of Non-Starchy Vegetables in place of the two tablespoons of Garden in My Glass. If you do not add more veggies and you do not add Garden in My Glass, track only two servings of Non-Starchy Vegetables per smoothie (instead of four servings).

**Only add protein if the smoothie is your entire meal. Vegetarians can use 6 TBSP of Clean Pea Protein (instead of Clean Whey Protein).

***To minimize sugar content, reduce fruit (other than lemon) and increase Slimming Sugar Substitute. If fruit is reduced by half or more, no Low-Fructose Fruit servings should be tracked. Due to their extremely low sugar content, lemons should not be reduced and do not need to be tracked.

PEACH NECTARINE DREAM

1 Serving   Prep: 1 min   Blend: 2 min   Total: 3 min
4 Non-Starchy Vegetables   1 Nutrient-Dense Protein   1 Low-Fructose Fruit

- 1/2 Cup Peach Slices (frozen or fresh)
- 1/2 Cup Nectarine Slices (frozen or fresh)
- 3 Cups Mixed Greens
- 3 Cups Spinach
- 1 Medium Lemon (peeled)
- 1/2 TSP Cinnamon
- 2 TBSP Garden in My Glass*
- 4 TBSP Clean Whey Protein**
- 1 TSP Hormone Healing Green Tea (optional)
- 2 TBSP Slimming Sugar Substitute (optional)***

DIRECTIONS

- Add all ingredients to a high-powered blender with 8 oz. cold water and a handful of ice.

- Blend for 2 minutes or until completely blended (i.e. no pieces of veggies or fruit are visible).

- Adjust the amount of water and ice for desired consistency and desired temperature.

TIP: Can't find some of these ingredients at your local grocery store? Have them delivered quickly and easily by visiting your SANE Superfoods Store at http://store.SANESolution.com.

NOTES

*You can add two additional serving of Non-Starchy Vegetables in place of the two tablespoons of Garden in My Glass. If you do not add more veggies and you do not add Garden in My Glass, track only two servings of Non-Starchy Vegetables per smoothie (instead of four servings).

**Only add protein if the smoothie is your entire meal. Vegetarians can use 6 TBSP of Clean Pea Protein (instead of Clean Whey Protein).

***To minimize sugar content, reduce fruit (other than lemon) and increase Slimming Sugar Substitute. If fruit is reduced by half or more, no Low-Fructose Fruit servings should be tracked. Due to their extremely low sugar content, lemons should not be reduced and do not need to be tracked.

PEACH ORANGE BLAST

1 Serving   Prep: 1 min   Blend: 2 min   Total: 3 min
4 Non-Starchy Vegetables   1 Nutrient-Dense Protein   1 Low-Fructose Fruit

- 1/2 Cup Peach Slices (frozen or fresh)
- 1/2 Medium Orange (peeled)
- 6 Cups Spinach
- 1 Medium Lemon (peeled)
- 1/2 TSP Cinnamon
- 2 TBSP Garden in My Glass*
- 4 TBSP Clean Whey Protein**
- 1 TSP Hormone Healing Green Tea (optional)
- 2 TBSP Slimming Sugar Substitute (optional)***

DIRECTIONS

- Add all ingredients to a high-powered blender with 8 oz. cold water and a handful of ice.

- Blend for 2 minutes or until completely blended (i.e. no pieces of veggies or fruit are visible).

- Adjust the amount of water and ice for desired consistency and desired temperature.

TIP: Can't find some of these ingredients at your local grocery store? Have them delivered quickly and easily by visiting your SANE Superfoods Store at http://store.SANESolution.com.

NOTES

*You can add two additional serving of Non-Starchy Vegetables in place of the two tablespoons of Garden in My Glass. If you do not add more veggies and you do not add Garden in My Glass, track only two servings of Non-Starchy Vegetables per smoothie (instead of four servings).

**Only add protein if the smoothie is your entire meal. Vegetarians can use 6 TBSP of Clean Pea Protein (instead of Clean Whey Protein).

***To minimize sugar content, reduce fruit (other than lemon) and increase Slimming Sugar Substitute. If fruit is reduced by half or more, no Low-Fructose Fruit servings should be tracked. Due to their extremely low sugar content, lemons should not be reduced and do not need to be tracked.

PEACH ORANGE BREEZE

1 Serving   Prep: 1 min   Blend: 2 min   Total: 3 min
4 Non-Starchy Vegetables   1 Nutrient-Dense Protein   1 Low-Fructose Fruit

- 1/2 Cup Peach Slices (frozen or fresh)
- 1/2 Medium Orange (peeled)
- 2 Cups Kale
- 4 Cups Romaine Lettuce
- 1 Medium Lemon (peeled)
- 1/2 TSP Cinnamon
- 2 TBSP Garden in My Glass*
- 4 TBSP Clean Whey Protein**
- 1 TSP Hormone Healing Green Tea (optional)
- 2 TBSP Slimming Sugar Substitute (optional)***

Directions

- Add all ingredients to a high-powered blender with 8 oz. cold water and a handful of ice.

- Blend for 2 minutes or until completely blended (i.e. no pieces of veggies or fruit are visible).

- Adjust the amount of water and ice for desired consistency and desired temperature.

TIP: Can't find some of these ingredients at your local grocery store? Have them delivered quickly and easily by visiting your SANE Superfoods Store at http://store.SANESolution.com.

Notes

*You can add two additional serving of Non-Starchy Vegetables in place of the two tablespoons of Garden in My Glass. If you do not add more veggies and you do not add Garden in My Glass, track only two servings of Non-Starchy Vegetables per smoothie (instead of four servings).

**Only add protein if the smoothie is your entire meal. Vegetarians can use 6 TBSP of Clean Pea Protein (instead of Clean Whey Protein).

***To minimize sugar content, reduce fruit (other than lemon) and increase Slimming Sugar Substitute. If fruit is reduced by half or more, no Low-Fructose Fruit servings should be tracked. Due to their extremely low sugar content, lemons should not be reduced and do not need to be tracked.

PEACH ORANGE SUNRISE

1 Serving   Prep: 1 min   Blend: 2 min   Total: 3 min
4 Non-Starchy Vegetables   1 Nutrient-Dense Protein   1 Low-Fructose Fruit

- 1/2 Cup Peach Slices (frozen or fresh)
- 1/2 Medium Orange (peeled)
- 6 Cups Romaine Lettuce
- 1 Medium Lemon (peeled)
- 1/2 TSP Cinnamon
- 2 TBSP Garden in My Glass*
- 4 TBSP Clean Whey Protein**
- 1 TSP Hormone Healing Green Tea (optional)
- 2 TBSP Slimming Sugar Substitute (optional)***

DIRECTIONS

- Add all ingredients to a high-powered blender with 8 oz. cold water and a handful of ice.

- Blend for 2 minutes or until completely blended (i.e. no pieces of veggies or fruit are visible).

- Adjust the amount of water and ice for desired consistency and desired temperature.

TIP: Can't find some of these ingredients at your local grocery store? Have them delivered quickly and easily by visiting your SANE Superfoods Store at http://store.SANESolution.com.

NOTES

*You can add two additional serving of Non-Starchy Vegetables in place of the two tablespoons of Garden in My Glass. If you do not add more veggies and you do not add Garden in My Glass, track only two servings of Non-Starchy Vegetables per smoothie (instead of four servings).

**Only add protein if the smoothie is your entire meal. Vegetarians can use 6 TBSP of Clean Pea Protein (instead of Clean Whey Protein).

***To minimize sugar content, reduce fruit (other than lemon) and increase Slimming Sugar Substitute. If fruit is reduced by half or more, no Low-Fructose Fruit servings should be tracked. Due to their extremely low sugar content, lemons should not be reduced and do not need to be tracked.

PEACH STRAWBERRY MAGIC

1 Serving   Prep: 1 min   Blend: 2 min   Total: 3 min
4 Non-Starchy Vegetables   1 Nutrient-Dense Protein   1 Low-Fructose Fruit

- 1/2 Cup Peach Slices (frozen or fresh)
- 1/2 Cup Strawberries (frozen or fresh)
- 2 Cups Arugula
- 4 Cups Spinach
- 1 Medium Lemon (peeled)
- 1/2 TSP Cinnamon
- 2 TBSP Garden in My Glass*
- 4 TBSP Clean Whey Protein**
- 1 TSP Hormone Healing Green Tea (optional)
- 2 TBSP Slimming Sugar Substitute (optional)***

DIRECTIONS

- Add all ingredients to a high-powered blender with 8 oz. cold water and a handful of ice.

- Blend for 2 minutes or until completely blended (i.e. no pieces of veggies or fruit are visible).

- Adjust the amount of water and ice for desired consistency and desired temperature.

TIP: Can't find some of these ingredients at your local grocery store? Have them delivered quickly and easily by visiting your SANE Superfoods Store at http://store.SANESolution.com.

NOTES

*You can add two additional serving of Non-Starchy Vegetables in place of the two tablespoons of Garden in My Glass. If you do not add more veggies and you do not add Garden in My Glass, track only two servings of Non-Starchy Vegetables per smoothie (instead of four servings).

**Only add protein if the smoothie is your entire meal. Vegetarians can use 6 TBSP of Clean Pea Protein (instead of Clean Whey Protein).

***To minimize sugar content, reduce fruit (other than lemon) and increase Slimming Sugar Substitute. If fruit is reduced by half or more, no Low-Fructose Fruit servings should be tracked. Due to their extremely low sugar content, lemons should not be reduced and do not need to be tracked.

PEACH STRAWBERRY SUNRISE

1 Serving   Prep: 1 min   Blend: 2 min   Total: 3 min
4 Non-Starchy Vegetables   1 Nutrient-Dense Protein   1 Low-Fructose Fruit

- 1/2 Cup Peach Slices (frozen or fresh)
- 1/2 Cup Strawberries (frozen or fresh)
- 6 Cups Romaine Lettuce
- 1 Medium Lemon (peeled)
- 1/2 TSP Cinnamon
- 2 TBSP Garden in My Glass*
- 4 TBSP Clean Whey Protein**
- 1 TSP Hormone Healing Green Tea (optional)
- 2 TBSP Slimming Sugar Substitute (optional)***

DIRECTIONS

- Add all ingredients to a high-powered blender with 8 oz. cold water and a handful of ice.

- Blend for 2 minutes or until completely blended (i.e. no pieces of veggies or fruit are visible).

- Adjust the amount of water and ice for desired consistency and desired temperature.

TIP: Can't find some of these ingredients at your local grocery store? Have them delivered quickly and easily by visiting your SANE Superfoods Store at http://store.SANESolution.com.

NOTES

*You can add two additional serving of Non-Starchy Vegetables in place of the two tablespoons of Garden in My Glass. If you do not add more veggies and you do not add Garden in My Glass, track only two servings of Non-Starchy Vegetables per smoothie (instead of four servings).

**Only add protein if the smoothie is your entire meal. Vegetarians can use 6 TBSP of Clean Pea Protein (instead of Clean Whey Protein).

***To minimize sugar content, reduce fruit (other than lemon) and increase Slimming Sugar Substitute. If fruit is reduced by half or more, no Low-Fructose Fruit servings should be tracked. Due to their extremely low sugar content, lemons should not be reduced and do not need to be tracked.

PEACH WHIRL

1 Serving   Prep: 1 min   Blend: 2 min   Total: 3 min
4 Non-Starchy Vegetables   1 Nutrient-Dense Protein   1 Low-Fructose Fruit

- 1 Cup Peach Slices (frozen or fresh)
- 3 Cups Spinach
- 3 Cups Romaine Lettuce
- 1 Medium Lemon (peeled)
- 1/2 TSP Cinnamon
- 2 TBSP Garden in My Glass*
- 4 TBSP Clean Whey Protein**
- 1 TSP Hormone Healing Green Tea (optional)
- 2 TBSP Slimming Sugar Substitute (optional)***

DIRECTIONS

- Add all ingredients to a high-powered blender with 8 oz. cold water and a handful of ice.

- Blend for 2 minutes or until completely blended (i.e. no pieces of veggies or fruit are visible).

- Adjust the amount of water and ice for desired consistency and desired temperature.

TIP: Can't find some of these ingredients at your local grocery store? Have them delivered quickly and easily by visiting your SANE Superfoods Store at http://store.SANESolution.com.

NOTES

*You can add two additional serving of Non-Starchy Vegetables in place of the two tablespoons of Garden in My Glass. If you do not add more veggies and you do not add Garden in My Glass, track only two servings of Non-Starchy Vegetables per smoothie (instead of four servings).

**Only add protein if the smoothie is your entire meal. Vegetarians can use 6 TBSP of Clean Pea Protein (instead of Clean Whey Protein).

***To minimize sugar content, reduce fruit (other than lemon) and increase Slimming Sugar Substitute. If fruit is reduced by half or more, no Low-Fructose Fruit servings should be tracked. Due to their extremely low sugar content, lemons should not be reduced and do not need to be tracked.

RASPBERRY BLISS

1 Serving   Prep: 1 min   Blend: 2 min   Total: 3 min

4 Non-Starchy Vegetables   1 Nutrient-Dense Protein   1 Low-Fructose Fruit

- 1 Cup Raspberries (frozen or fresh)
- 2 Cups Arugula
- 4 Cups Romaine Lettuce
- 1 Medium Lemon (peeled)
- 1/2 TSP Cinnamon
- 2 TBSP Garden in My Glass*
- 4 TBSP Clean Whey Protein**
- 1 TSP Hormone Healing Green Tea (optional)
- 2 TBSP Slimming Sugar Substitute (optional)***

DIRECTIONS

- Add all ingredients to a high-powered blender with 8 oz. cold water and a handful of ice.

- Blend for 2 minutes or until completely blended (i.e. no pieces of veggies or fruit are visible).

- Adjust the amount of water and ice for desired consistency and desired temperature.

TIP: Can't find some of these ingredients at your local grocery store? Have them delivered quickly and easily by visiting your SANE Superfoods Store at http://store.SANESolution.com.

NOTES

*You can add two additional serving of Non-Starchy Vegetables in place of the two tablespoons of Garden in My Glass. If you do not add more veggies and you do not add Garden in My Glass, track only two servings of Non-Starchy Vegetables per smoothie (instead of four servings).

**Only add protein if the smoothie is your entire meal. Vegetarians can use 6 TBSP of Clean Pea Protein (instead of Clean Whey Protein).

***To minimize sugar content, reduce fruit (other than lemon) and increase Slimming Sugar Substitute. If fruit is reduced by half or more, no Low-Fructose Fruit servings should be tracked. Due to their extremely low sugar content, lemons should not be reduced and do not need to be tracked.

RASPBERRY CRANBERRY BREEZE

1 Serving   Prep: 1 min   Blend: 2 min   Total: 3 min
4 Non-Starchy Vegetables   1 Nutrient-Dense Protein   1 Low-Fructose Fruit

- 3/4 Cup Raspberries (frozen or fresh)
- 1 Cup Pitted Cranberries (frozen or fresh)
- 2 Cups Kale
- 4 Cups Romaine Lettuce
- 1 Medium Lemon (peeled)
- 1/2 TSP Cinnamon
- 2 TBSP Garden in My Glass*
- 4 TBSP Clean Whey Protein**
- 1 TSP Hormone Healing Green Tea (optional)
- 2 TBSP Slimming Sugar Substitute (optional)***

DIRECTIONS

- Add all ingredients to a high-powered blender with 8 oz. cold water and a handful of ice.

- Blend for 2 minutes or until completely blended (i.e. no pieces of veggies or fruit are visible).

- Adjust the amount of water and ice for desired consistency and desired temperature.

TIP: Can't find some of these ingredients at your local grocery store? Have them delivered quickly and easily by visiting your SANE Superfoods Store at http://store.SANESolution.com.

NOTES

*You can add two additional serving of Non-Starchy Vegetables in place of the two tablespoons of Garden in My Glass. If you do not add more veggies and you do not add Garden in My Glass, track only two servings of Non-Starchy Vegetables per smoothie (instead of four servings).

**Only add protein if the smoothie is your entire meal. Vegetarians can use 6 TBSP of Clean Pea Protein (instead of Clean Whey Protein).

***To minimize sugar content, reduce fruit (other than lemon) and increase Slimming Sugar Substitute. If fruit is reduced by half or more, no Low-Fructose Fruit servings should be tracked. Due to their extremely low sugar content, lemons should not be reduced and do not need to be tracked.

RASPBERRY CRANBERRY ESCAPE

1 Serving   Prep: 1 min   Blend: 2 min   Total: 3 min
4 Non-Starchy Vegetables   1 Nutrient-Dense Protein   1 Low-Fructose Fruit

- 3/4 Cup Raspberries (frozen or fresh)
- 1 Cup Pitted Cranberries (frozen or fresh)
- 2 Cups Chard
- 4 Cups Spinach
- 1 Medium Lemon (peeled)
- 1/2 TSP Cinnamon
- 2 TBSP Garden in My Glass*
- 4 TBSP Clean Whey Protein**
- 1 TSP Hormone Healing Green Tea (optional)
- 2 TBSP Slimming Sugar Substitute (optional)***

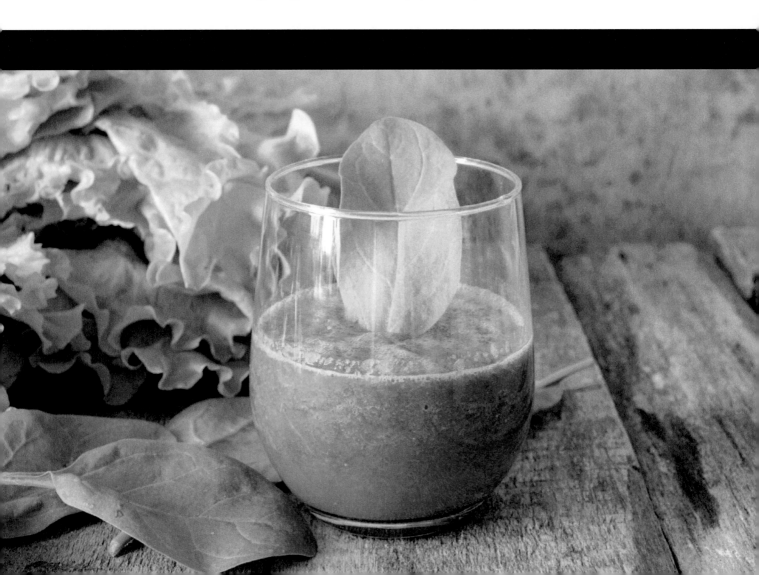

DIRECTIONS

- Add all ingredients to a high-powered blender with 8 oz. cold water and a handful of ice.

- Blend for 2 minutes or until completely blended (i.e. no pieces of veggies or fruit are visible).

- Adjust the amount of water and ice for desired consistency and desired temperature.

TIP: Can't find some of these ingredients at your local grocery store? Have them delivered quickly and easily by visiting your SANE Superfoods Store at http://store.SANESolution.com.

NOTES

*You can add two additional serving of Non-Starchy Vegetables in place of the two tablespoons of Garden in My Glass. If you do not add more veggies and you do not add Garden in My Glass, track only two servings of Non-Starchy Vegetables per smoothie (instead of four servings).

**Only add protein if the smoothie is your entire meal. Vegetarians can use 6 TBSP of Clean Pea Protein (instead of Clean Whey Protein).

***To minimize sugar content, reduce fruit (other than lemon) and increase Slimming Sugar Substitute. If fruit is reduced by half or more, no Low-Fructose Fruit servings should be tracked. Due to their extremely low sugar content, lemons should not be reduced and do not need to be tracked.

RASPBERRY CRANBERRY WHIRL

1 Serving   Prep: 1 min   Blend: 2 min   Total: 3 min
4 Non-Starchy Vegetables   1 Nutrient-Dense Protein   1 Low-Fructose Fruit

- 3/4 Cup Raspberries (frozen or fresh)
- 1 Cup Pitted Cranberries (frozen or fresh)
- 3 Cups Spinach
- 3 Cups Romaine Lettuce
- 1 Medium Lemon (peeled)
- 1/2 TSP Cinnamon
- 2 TBSP Garden in My Glass*
- 4 TBSP Clean Whey Protein**
- 1 TSP Hormone Healing Green Tea (optional)
- 2 TBSP Slimming Sugar Substitute (optional)***

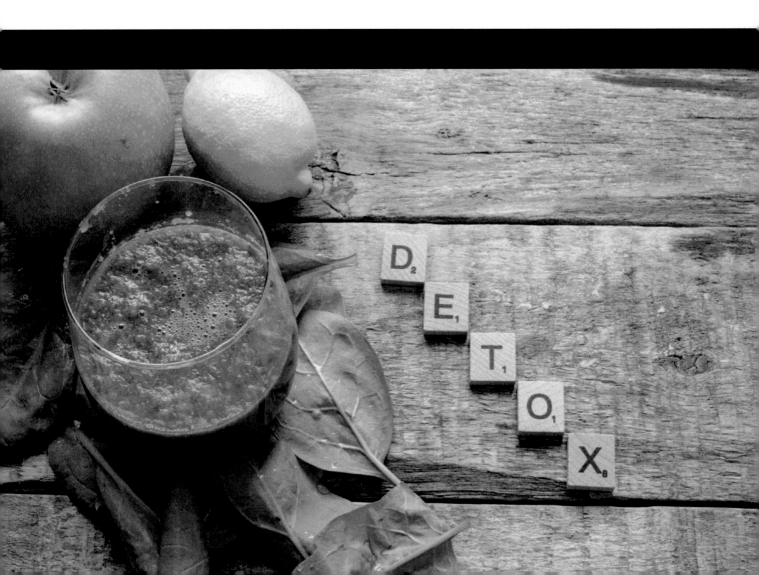

DIRECTIONS

- Add all ingredients to a high-powered blender with 8 oz. cold water and a handful of ice.

- Blend for 2 minutes or until completely blended (i.e. no pieces of veggies or fruit are visible).

- Adjust the amount of water and ice for desired consistency and desired temperature.

TIP: Can't find some of these ingredients at your local grocery store? Have them delivered quickly and easily by visiting your SANE Superfoods Store at http://store.SANESolution.com.

NOTES

*You can add two additional serving of Non-Starchy Vegetables in place of the two tablespoons of Garden in My Glass. If you do not add more veggies and you do not add Garden in My Glass, track only two servings of Non-Starchy Vegetables per smoothie (instead of four servings).

**Only add protein if the smoothie is your entire meal. Vegetarians can use 6 TBSP of Clean Pea Protein (instead of Clean Whey Protein).

***To minimize sugar content, reduce fruit (other than lemon) and increase Slimming Sugar Substitute. If fruit is reduced by half or more, no Low-Fructose Fruit servings should be tracked. Due to their extremely low sugar content, lemons should not be reduced and do not need to be tracked.

RASPBERRY GLEE

1 Serving   Prep: 1 min   Blend: 2 min   Total: 3 min
4 Non-Starchy Vegetables   1 Nutrient-Dense Protein   1 Low-Fructose Fruit

- 1 Cup Raspberries (frozen or fresh)
- 2 Cups Chard
- 4 Cups Romaine Lettuce
- 1 Medium Lemon (peeled)
- 1/2 TSP Cinnamon
- 2 TBSP Garden in My Glass*
- 4 TBSP Clean Whey Protein**
- 1 TSP Hormone Healing Green Tea (optional)
- 2 TBSP Slimming Sugar Substitute (optional)***

DIRECTIONS

- Add all ingredients to a high-powered blender with 8 oz. cold water and a handful of ice.

- Blend for 2 minutes or until completely blended (i.e. no pieces of veggies or fruit are visible).

- Adjust the amount of water and ice for desired consistency and desired temperature.

TIP: Can't find some of these ingredients at your local grocery store? Have them delivered quickly and easily by visiting your SANE Superfoods Store at http://store.SANESolution.com.

NOTES

*You can add two additional serving of Non-Starchy Vegetables in place of the two tablespoons of Garden in My Glass. If you do not add more veggies and you do not add Garden in My Glass, track only two servings of Non-Starchy Vegetables per smoothie (instead of four servings).

**Only add protein if the smoothie is your entire meal. Vegetarians can use 6 TBSP of Clean Pea Protein (instead of Clean Whey Protein).

***To minimize sugar content, reduce fruit (other than lemon) and increase Slimming Sugar Substitute. If fruit is reduced by half or more, no Low-Fructose Fruit servings should be tracked. Due to their extremely low sugar content, lemons should not be reduced and do not need to be tracked.

RASPBERRY ORANGE BLISS

1 Serving   Prep: 1 min   Blend: 2 min   Total: 3 min
4 Non-Starchy Vegetables   1 Nutrient-Dense Protein   1 Low-Fructose Fruit

- 3/4 Cup Raspberries (frozen or fresh)
- 1/2 Medium Orange (peeled)
- 2 Cups Arugula
- 4 Cups Romaine Lettuce
- 1 Medium Lemon (peeled)
- 1/2 TSP Cinnamon
- 2 TBSP Garden in My Glass*
- 4 TBSP Clean Whey Protein**
- 1 TSP Hormone Healing Green Tea (optional)
- 2 TBSP Slimming Sugar Substitute (optional)***

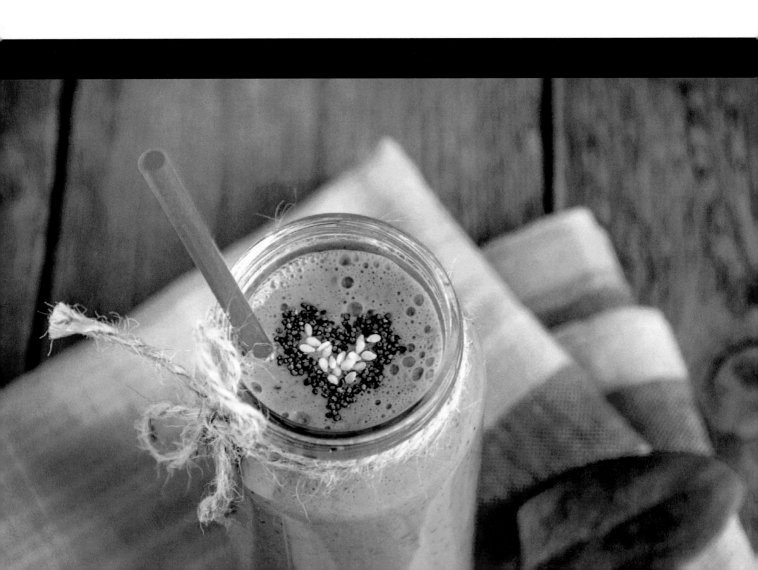

DIRECTIONS

- Add all ingredients to a high-powered blender with 8 oz. cold water and a handful of ice.

- Blend for 2 minutes or until completely blended (i.e. no pieces of veggies or fruit are visible).

- Adjust the amount of water and ice for desired consistency and desired temperature.

TIP: Can't find some of these ingredients at your local grocery store? Have them delivered quickly and easily by visiting your SANE Superfoods Store at http://store.SANESolution.com.

NOTES

*You can add two additional serving of Non-Starchy Vegetables in place of the two tablespoons of Garden in My Glass. If you do not add more veggies and you do not add Garden in My Glass, track only two servings of Non-Starchy Vegetables per smoothie (instead of four servings).

**Only add protein if the smoothie is your entire meal. Vegetarians can use 6 TBSP of Clean Pea Protein (instead of Clean Whey Protein).

***To minimize sugar content, reduce fruit (other than lemon) and increase Slimming Sugar Substitute. If fruit is reduced by half or more, no Low-Fructose Fruit servings should be tracked. Due to their extremely low sugar content, lemons should not be reduced and do not need to be tracked.

RASPBERRY ORANGE GLEE

1 Serving   Prep: 1 min   Blend: 2 min   Total: 3 min
4 Non-Starchy Vegetables   1 Nutrient-Dense Protein   1 Low-Fructose Fruit

- 3/4 Cup Raspberries (frozen or fresh)
- 1/2 Medium Orange (peeled)
- 2 Cups Chard
- 4 Cups Romaine Lettuce
- 1 Medium Lemon (peeled)
- 1/2 TSP Cinnamon
- 2 TBSP Garden in My Glass*
- 4 TBSP Clean Whey Protein**
- 1 TSP Hormone Healing Green Tea (optional)
- 2 TBSP Slimming Sugar Substitute (optional)***

DIRECTIONS

- Add all ingredients to a high-powered blender with 8 oz. cold water and a handful of ice.

- Blend for 2 minutes or until completely blended (i.e. no pieces of veggies or fruit are visible).

- Adjust the amount of water and ice for desired consistency and desired temperature.

TIP: Can't find some of these ingredients at your local grocery store? Have them delivered quickly and easily by visiting your SANE Superfoods Store at http://store.SANESolution.com.

NOTES

*You can add two additional serving of Non-Starchy Vegetables in place of the two tablespoons of Garden in My Glass. If you do not add more veggies and you do not add Garden in My Glass, track only two servings of Non-Starchy Vegetables per smoothie (instead of four servings).

**Only add protein if the smoothie is your entire meal. Vegetarians can use 6 TBSP of Clean Pea Protein (instead of Clean Whey Protein).

***To minimize sugar content, reduce fruit (other than lemon) and increase Slimming Sugar Substitute. If fruit is reduced by half or more, no Low-Fructose Fruit servings should be tracked. Due to their extremely low sugar content, lemons should not be reduced and do not need to be tracked.

RASPBERRY ORANGE MAGIC

1 Serving   Prep: 1 min   Blend: 2 min   Total: 3 min
4 Non-Starchy Vegetables   1 Nutrient-Dense Protein   1 Low-Fructose Fruit

- 3/4 Cup Raspberries (frozen or fresh)
- 1/2 Medium Orange (peeled)
- 2 Cups Arugula
- 4 Cups Spinach
- 1 Medium Lemon (peeled)
- 1/2 TSP Cinnamon
- 2 TBSP Garden in My Glass*
- 4 TBSP Clean Whey Protein**
- 1 TSP Hormone Healing Green Tea (optional)
- 2 TBSP Slimming Sugar Substitute (optional)***

DIRECTIONS

- Add all ingredients to a high-powered blender with 8 oz. cold water and a handful of ice.

- Blend for 2 minutes or until completely blended (i.e. no pieces of veggies or fruit are visible).

- Adjust the amount of water and ice for desired consistency and desired temperature.

TIP: Can't find some of these ingredients at your local grocery store? Have them delivered quickly and easily by visiting your SANE Superfoods Store at http://store.SANESolution.com.

NOTES

*You can add two additional serving of Non-Starchy Vegetables in place of the two tablespoons of Garden in My Glass. If you do not add more veggies and you do not add Garden in My Glass, track only two servings of Non-Starchy Vegetables per smoothie (instead of four servings).

**Only add protein if the smoothie is your entire meal. Vegetarians can use 6 TBSP of Clean Pea Protein (instead of Clean Whey Protein).

***To minimize sugar content, reduce fruit (other than lemon) and increase Slimming Sugar Substitute. If fruit is reduced by half or more, no Low-Fructose Fruit servings should be tracked. Due to their extremely low sugar content, lemons should not be reduced and do not need to be tracked.

RASPBERRY ORANGE WHIRL

1 Serving   Prep: 1 min   Blend: 2 min   Total: 3 min
4 Non-Starchy Vegetables   1 Nutrient-Dense Protein   1 Low-Fructose Fruit

- 3/4 Cup Raspberries (frozen or fresh)
- 1/2 Medium Orange (peeled)
- 3 Cups Spinach
- 3 Cups Romaine Lettuce
- 1 Medium Lemon (peeled)
- 1/2 TSP Cinnamon
- 2 TBSP Garden in My Glass*
- 4 TBSP Clean Whey Protein**
- 1 TSP Hormone Healing Green Tea (optional)
- 2 TBSP Slimming Sugar Substitute (optional)***

Directions

- Add all ingredients to a high-powered blender with 8 oz. cold water and a handful of ice.

- Blend for 2 minutes or until completely blended (i.e. no pieces of veggies or fruit are visible).

- Adjust the amount of water and ice for desired consistency and desired temperature.

TIP: Can't find some of these ingredients at your local grocery store? Have them delivered quickly and easily by visiting your SANE Superfoods Store at http://store.SANESolution.com.

Notes

*You can add two additional serving of Non-Starchy Vegetables in place of the two tablespoons of Garden in My Glass. If you do not add more veggies and you do not add Garden in My Glass, track only two servings of Non-Starchy Vegetables per smoothie (instead of four servings).

**Only add protein if the smoothie is your entire meal. Vegetarians can use 6 TBSP of Clean Pea Protein (instead of Clean Whey Protein).

***To minimize sugar content, reduce fruit (other than lemon) and increase Slimming Sugar Substitute. If fruit is reduced by half or more, no Low-Fructose Fruit servings should be tracked. Due to their extremely low sugar content, lemons should not be reduced and do not need to be tracked.

RASPBERRY SUNRISE

1 Serving   Prep: 1 min   Blend: 2 min   Total: 3 min
4 Non-Starchy Vegetables   1 Nutrient-Dense Protein   1 Low-Fructose Fruit

- 1 Cup Raspberries (frozen or fresh)
- 6 Cups Romaine Lettuce
- 1 Medium Lemon (peeled)
- 1/2 TSP Cinnamon
- 2 TBSP Garden in My Glass*
- 4 TBSP Clean Whey Protein**
- 1 TSP Hormone Healing Green Tea (optional)
- 2 TBSP Slimming Sugar Substitute (optional)***

DIRECTIONS

- Add all ingredients to a high-powered blender with 8 oz. cold water and a handful of ice.

- Blend for 2 minutes or until completely blended (i.e. no pieces of veggies or fruit are visible).

- Adjust the amount of water and ice for desired consistency and desired temperature.

TIP: Can't find some of these ingredients at your local grocery store? Have them delivered quickly and easily by visiting your SANE Superfoods Store at http://store.SANESolution.com.

NOTES

*You can add two additional serving of Non-Starchy Vegetables in place of the two tablespoons of Garden in My Glass. If you do not add more veggies and you do not add Garden in My Glass, track only two servings of Non-Starchy Vegetables per smoothie (instead of four servings).

**Only add protein if the smoothie is your entire meal. Vegetarians can use 6 TBSP of Clean Pea Protein (instead of Clean Whey Protein).

***To minimize sugar content, reduce fruit (other than lemon) and increase Slimming Sugar Substitute. If fruit is reduced by half or more, no Low-Fructose Fruit servings should be tracked. Due to their extremely low sugar content, lemons should not be reduced and do not need to be tracked.

RASPBERRY WHIRL

1 Serving   Prep: 1 min   Blend: 2 min   Total: 3 min
4 Non-Starchy Vegetables   1 Nutrient-Dense Protein   1 Low-Fructose Fruit

- 1 Cup Raspberries (frozen or fresh)
- 3 Cups Spinach
- 3 Cups Romaine Lettuce
- 1 Medium Lemon (peeled)
- 1/2 TSP Cinnamon
- 2 TBSP Garden in My Glass*
- 4 TBSP Clean Whey Protein**
- 1 TSP Hormone Healing Green Tea (optional)
- 2 TBSP Slimming Sugar Substitute (optional)***

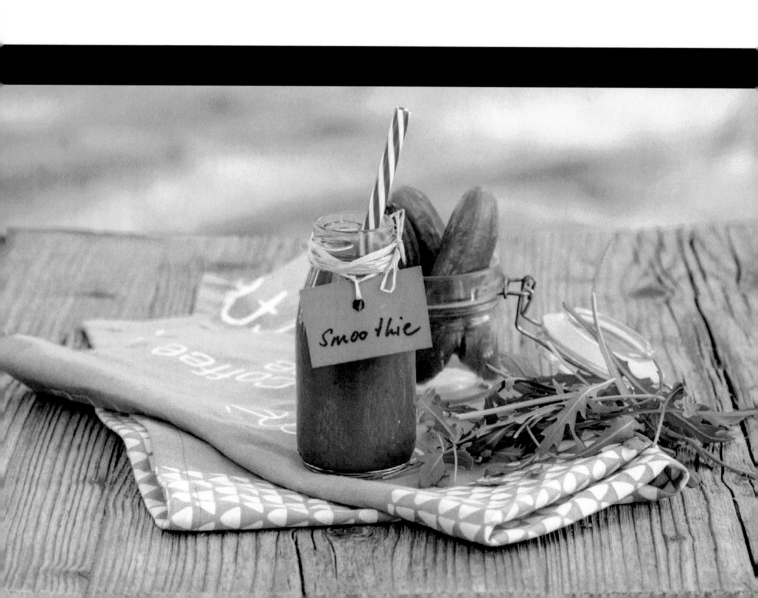

Directions

- Add all ingredients to a high-powered blender with 8 oz. cold water and a handful of ice.

- Blend for 2 minutes or until completely blended (i.e. no pieces of veggies or fruit are visible).

- Adjust the amount of water and ice for desired consistency and desired temperature.

TIP: Can't find some of these ingredients at your local grocery store? Have them delivered quickly and easily by visiting your SANE Superfoods Store at http://store.SANESolution.com.

Notes

*You can add two additional serving of Non-Starchy Vegetables in place of the two tablespoons of Garden in My Glass. If you do not add more veggies and you do not add Garden in My Glass, track only two servings of Non-Starchy Vegetables per smoothie (instead of four servings).

**Only add protein if the smoothie is your entire meal. Vegetarians can use 6 TBSP of Clean Pea Protein (instead of Clean Whey Protein).

***To minimize sugar content, reduce fruit (other than lemon) and increase Slimming Sugar Substitute. If fruit is reduced by half or more, no Low-Fructose Fruit servings should be tracked. Due to their extremely low sugar content, lemons should not be reduced and do not need to be tracked.

STRAWBERRY BLUEBERRY BLAST

1 Serving   Prep: 1 min   Blend: 2 min   Total: 3 min
4 Non-Starchy Vegetables   1 Nutrient-Dense Protein   1 Low-Fructose Fruit

- 1/2 Cup Strawberries (frozen or fresh)
- 1/3 Cup Blueberries (frozen or fresh)
- 6 Cups Spinach
- 1 Medium Lemon (peeled)
- 1/2 TSP Cinnamon
- 2 TBSP Garden in My Glass*
- 4 TBSP Clean Whey Protein**
- 1 TSP Hormone Healing Green Tea (optional)
- 2 TBSP Slimming Sugar Substitute (optional)***

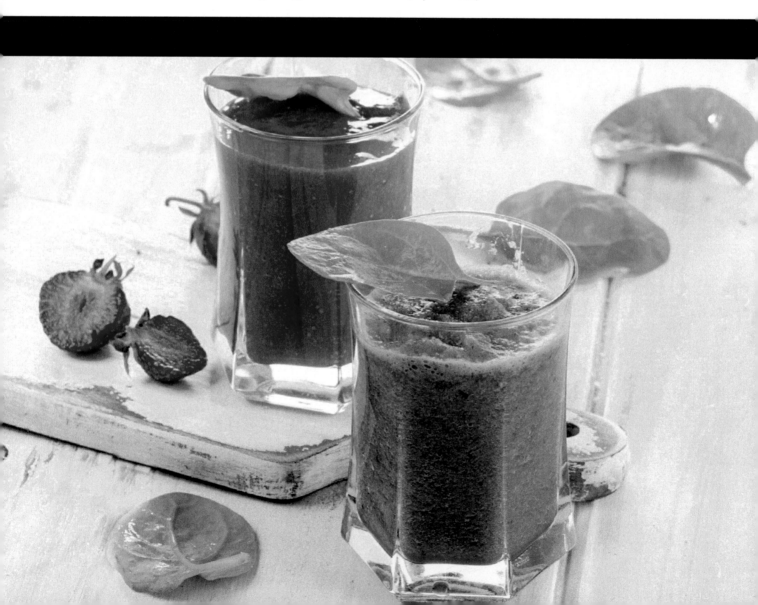

DIRECTIONS

- Add all ingredients to a high-powered blender with 8 oz. cold water and a handful of ice.

- Blend for 2 minutes or until completely blended (i.e. no pieces of veggies or fruit are visible).

- Adjust the amount of water and ice for desired consistency and desired temperature.

TIP: Can't find some of these ingredients at your local grocery store? Have them delivered quickly and easily by visiting your SANE Superfoods Store at http://store.SANESolution.com.

NOTES

*You can add two additional serving of Non-Starchy Vegetables in place of the two tablespoons of Garden in My Glass. If you do not add more veggies and you do not add Garden in My Glass, track only two servings of Non-Starchy Vegetables per smoothie (instead of four servings).

**Only add protein if the smoothie is your entire meal. Vegetarians can use 6 TBSP of Clean Pea Protein (instead of Clean Whey Protein).

***To minimize sugar content, reduce fruit (other than lemon) and increase Slimming Sugar Substitute. If fruit is reduced by half or more, no Low-Fructose Fruit servings should be tracked. Due to their extremely low sugar content, lemons should not be reduced and do not need to be tracked.

STRAWBERRY BLUEBERRY ESCAPE

1 Serving   Prep: 1 min   Blend: 2 min   Total: 3 min
4 Non-Starchy Vegetables   1 Nutrient-Dense Protein   1 Low-Fructose Fruit

- 1/2 Cup Strawberries (frozen or fresh)
- 1/3 Cup Blueberries (frozen or fresh)
- 2 Cups Chard
- 4 Cups Spinach
- 1 Medium Lemon (peeled)
- 1/2 TSP Cinnamon
- 2 TBSP Garden in My Glass*
- 4 TBSP Clean Whey Protein**
- 1 TSP Hormone Healing Green Tea (optional)
- 2 TBSP Slimming Sugar Substitute (optional)***

DIRECTIONS

- Add all ingredients to a high-powered blender with 8 oz. cold water and a handful of ice.

- Blend for 2 minutes or until completely blended (i.e. no pieces of veggies or fruit are visible).

- Adjust the amount of water and ice for desired consistency and desired temperature.

TIP: Can't find some of these ingredients at your local grocery store? Have them delivered quickly and easily by visiting your SANE Superfoods Store at http://store.SANESolution.com.

NOTES

*You can add two additional serving of Non-Starchy Vegetables in place of the two tablespoons of Garden in My Glass. If you do not add more veggies and you do not add Garden in My Glass, track only two servings of Non-Starchy Vegetables per smoothie (instead of four servings).

**Only add protein if the smoothie is your entire meal. Vegetarians can use 6 TBSP of Clean Pea Protein (instead of Clean Whey Protein).

***To minimize sugar content, reduce fruit (other than lemon) and increase Slimming Sugar Substitute. If fruit is reduced by half or more, no Low-Fructose Fruit servings should be tracked. Due to their extremely low sugar content, lemons should not be reduced and do not need to be tracked.

STRAWBERRY BLUEBERRY MAGIC

1 Serving   Prep: 1 min   Blend: 2 min   Total: 3 min
4 Non-Starchy Vegetables   1 Nutrient-Dense Protein   1 Low-Fructose Fruit

- 1/2 Cup Strawberries (frozen or fresh)
- 1/3 Cup Blueberries (frozen or fresh)
- 2 Cups Arugula
- 4 Cups Spinach
- 1 Medium Lemon (peeled)
- 1/2 TSP Cinnamon
- 2 TBSP Garden in My Glass*
- 4 TBSP Clean Whey Protein**
- 1 TSP Hormone Healing Green Tea (optional)
- 2 TBSP Slimming Sugar Substitute (optional)***

DIRECTIONS

- Add all ingredients to a high-powered blender with 8 oz. cold water and a handful of ice.

- Blend for 2 minutes or until completely blended (i.e. no pieces of veggies or fruit are visible).

- Adjust the amount of water and ice for desired consistency and desired temperature.

TIP: Can't find some of these ingredients at your local grocery store? Have them delivered quickly and easily by visiting your SANE Superfoods Store at http://store.SANESolution.com.

NOTES

*You can add two additional serving of Non-Starchy Vegetables in place of the two tablespoons of Garden in My Glass. If you do not add more veggies and you do not add Garden in My Glass, track only two servings of Non-Starchy Vegetables per smoothie (instead of four servings).

**Only add protein if the smoothie is your entire meal. Vegetarians can use 6 TBSP of Clean Pea Protein (instead of Clean Whey Protein).

***To minimize sugar content, reduce fruit (other than lemon) and increase Slimming Sugar Substitute. If fruit is reduced by half or more, no Low-Fructose Fruit servings should be tracked. Due to their extremely low sugar content, lemons should not be reduced and do not need to be tracked.

STRAWBERRY BLUEBERRY WHIRL

1 Serving   Prep: 1 min   Blend: 2 min   Total: 3 min
4 Non-Starchy Vegetables   1 Nutrient-Dense Protein   1 Low-Fructose Fruit

- 1/2 Cup Strawberries (frozen or fresh)
- 1/3 Cup Blueberries (frozen or fresh)
- 3 Cups Spinach
- 3 Cups Romaine Lettuce
- 1 Medium Lemon (peeled)
- 1/2 TSP Cinnamon
- 2 TBSP Garden in My Glass*
- 4 TBSP Clean Whey Protein**
- 1 TSP Hormone Healing Green Tea (optional)
- 2 TBSP Slimming Sugar Substitute (optional)***

Directions

- Add all ingredients to a high-powered blender with 8 oz. cold water and a handful of ice.

- Blend for 2 minutes or until completely blended (i.e. no pieces of veggies or fruit are visible).

- Adjust the amount of water and ice for desired consistency and desired temperature.

TIP: Can't find some of these ingredients at your local grocery store? Have them delivered quickly and easily by visiting your SANE Superfoods Store at http://store.SANESolution.com.

Notes

*You can add two additional serving of Non-Starchy Vegetables in place of the two tablespoons of Garden in My Glass. If you do not add more veggies and you do not add Garden in My Glass, track only two servings of Non-Starchy Vegetables per smoothie (instead of four servings).

**Only add protein if the smoothie is your entire meal. Vegetarians can use 6 TBSP of Clean Pea Protein (instead of Clean Whey Protein).

***To minimize sugar content, reduce fruit (other than lemon) and increase Slimming Sugar Substitute. If fruit is reduced by half or more, no Low-Fructose Fruit servings should be tracked. Due to their extremely low sugar content, lemons should not be reduced and do not need to be tracked.

STRAWBERRY BREEZE

1 Serving   Prep: 1 min   Blend: 2 min   Total: 3 min
4 Non-Starchy Vegetables   1 Nutrient-Dense Protein   1 Low-Fructose Fruit

- 1 Cup Strawberries (frozen or fresh)
- 2 Cups Kale
- 4 Cups Romaine Lettuce
- 1 Medium Lemon (peeled)
- 1/2 TSP Cinnamon
- 2 TBSP Garden in My Glass*
- 4 TBSP Clean Whey Protein**
- 1 TSP Hormone Healing Green Tea (optional)
- 2 TBSP Slimming Sugar Substitute (optional)***

DIRECTIONS

- Add all ingredients to a high-powered blender with 8 oz. cold water and a handful of ice.

- Blend for 2 minutes or until completely blended (i.e. no pieces of veggies or fruit are visible).

- Adjust the amount of water and ice for desired consistency and desired temperature.

TIP: Can't find some of these ingredients at your local grocery store? Have them delivered quickly and easily by visiting your SANE Superfoods Store at http://store.SANESolution.com.

NOTES

*You can add two additional serving of Non-Starchy Vegetables in place of the two tablespoons of Garden in My Glass. If you do not add more veggies and you do not add Garden in My Glass, track only two servings of Non-Starchy Vegetables per smoothie (instead of four servings).

**Only add protein if the smoothie is your entire meal. Vegetarians can use 6 TBSP of Clean Pea Protein (instead of Clean Whey Protein).

***To minimize sugar content, reduce fruit (other than lemon) and increase Slimming Sugar Substitute. If fruit is reduced by half or more, no Low-Fructose Fruit servings should be tracked. Due to their extremely low sugar content, lemons should not be reduced and do not need to be tracked.

STRAWBERRY GLEE

1 Serving   Prep: 1 min   Blend: 2 min   Total: 3 min
4 Non-Starchy Vegetables   1 Nutrient-Dense Protein   1 Low-Fructose Fruit

- 1 Cup Strawberries (frozen or fresh)
- 2 Cups Chard
- 4 Cups Romaine Lettuce
- 1 Medium Lemon (peeled)
- 1/2 TSP Cinnamon
- 2 TBSP Garden in My Glass*
- 4 TBSP Clean Whey Protein**
- 1 TSP Hormone Healing Green Tea (optional)
- 2 TBSP Slimming Sugar Substitute (optional)***

DIRECTIONS

- Add all ingredients to a high-powered blender with 8 oz. cold water and a handful of ice.

- Blend for 2 minutes or until completely blended (i.e. no pieces of veggies or fruit are visible).

- Adjust the amount of water and ice for desired consistency and desired temperature.

TIP: Can't find some of these ingredients at your local grocery store? Have them delivered quickly and easily by visiting your SANE Superfoods Store at http://store.SANESolution.com.

NOTES

*You can add two additional serving of Non-Starchy Vegetables in place of the two tablespoons of Garden in My Glass. If you do not add more veggies and you do not add Garden in My Glass, track only two servings of Non-Starchy Vegetables per smoothie (instead of four servings).

**Only add protein if the smoothie is your entire meal. Vegetarians can use 6 TBSP of Clean Pea Protein (instead of Clean Whey Protein).

***To minimize sugar content, reduce fruit (other than lemon) and increase Slimming Sugar Substitute. If fruit is reduced by half or more, no Low-Fructose Fruit servings should be tracked. Due to their extremely low sugar content, lemons should not be reduced and do not need to be tracked.

STRAWBERRY GRAPEFRUIT BREEZE

1 Serving   Prep: 1 min   Blend: 2 min   Total: 3 min
4 Non-Starchy Vegetables   1 Nutrient-Dense Protein   1 Low-Fructose Fruit

- 1/2 Cup Strawberries (frozen or fresh)
- 1/2 Medium Grapefruit (peeled)
- 2 Cups Kale
- 4 Cups Romaine Lettuce
- 1 Medium Lemon (peeled)
- 1/2 TSP Cinnamon
- 2 TBSP Garden in My Glass*
- 4 TBSP Clean Whey Protein**
- 1 TSP Hormone Healing Green Tea (optional)
- 2 TBSP Slimming Sugar Substitute (optional)***

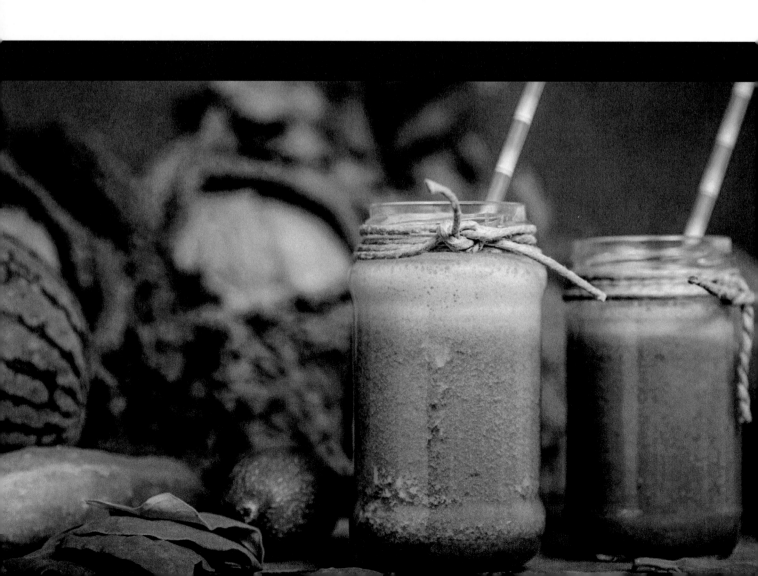

Directions

- Add all ingredients to a high-powered blender with 8 oz. cold water and a handful of ice.

- Blend for 2 minutes or until completely blended (i.e. no pieces of veggies or fruit are visible).

- Adjust the amount of water and ice for desired consistency and desired temperature.

TIP: Can't find some of these ingredients at your local grocery store? Have them delivered quickly and easily by visiting your SANE Superfoods Store at http://store.SANESolution.com.

Notes

*You can add two additional serving of Non-Starchy Vegetables in place of the two tablespoons of Garden in My Glass. If you do not add more veggies and you do not add Garden in My Glass, track only two servings of Non-Starchy Vegetables per smoothie (instead of four servings).

**Only add protein if the smoothie is your entire meal. Vegetarians can use 6 TBSP of Clean Pea Protein (instead of Clean Whey Protein).

***To minimize sugar content, reduce fruit (other than lemon) and increase Slimming Sugar Substitute. If fruit is reduced by half or more, no Low-Fructose Fruit servings should be tracked. Due to their extremely low sugar content, lemons should not be reduced and do not need to be tracked.

STRAWBERRY GRAPEFRUIT MAGIC

1 Serving   Prep: 1 min   Blend: 2 min   Total: 3 min
4 Non-Starchy Vegetables   1 Nutrient-Dense Protein   1 Low-Fructose Fruit

- 1/2 Cup Strawberries (frozen or fresh)
- 1/2 Medium Grapefruit (peeled)
- 2 Cups Arugula
- 4 Cups Spinach
- 1 Medium Lemon (peeled)
- 1/2 TSP Cinnamon
- 2 TBSP Garden in My Glass*
- 4 TBSP Clean Whey Protein**
- 1 TSP Hormone Healing Green Tea (optional)
- 2 TBSP Slimming Sugar Substitute (optional)***

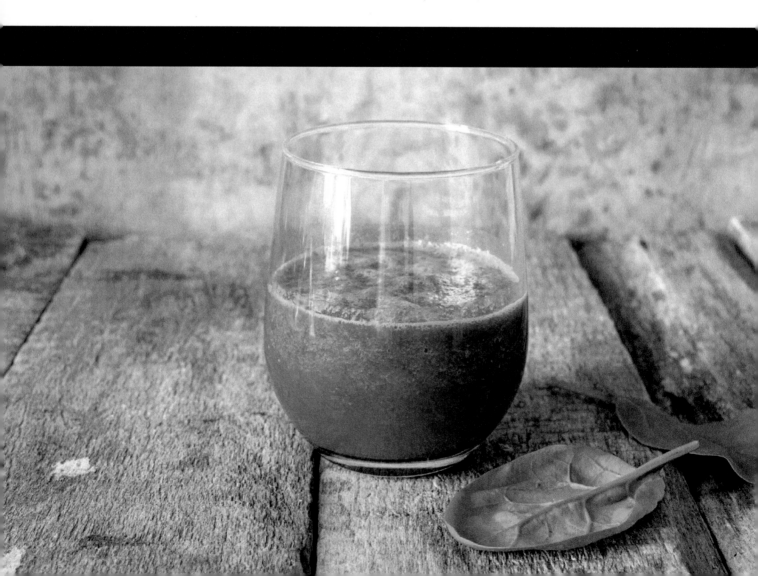

Directions

- Add all ingredients to a high-powered blender with 8 oz. cold water and a handful of ice.

- Blend for 2 minutes or until completely blended (i.e. no pieces of veggies or fruit are visible).

- Adjust the amount of water and ice for desired consistency and desired temperature.

TIP: Can't find some of these ingredients at your local grocery store? Have them delivered quickly and easily by visiting your SANE Superfoods Store at http://store.SANESolution.com.

Notes

*You can add two additional serving of Non-Starchy Vegetables in place of the two tablespoons of Garden in My Glass. If you do not add more veggies and you do not add Garden in My Glass, track only two servings of Non-Starchy Vegetables per smoothie (instead of four servings).

**Only add protein if the smoothie is your entire meal. Vegetarians can use 6 TBSP of Clean Pea Protein (instead of Clean Whey Protein).

***To minimize sugar content, reduce fruit (other than lemon) and increase Slimming Sugar Substitute. If fruit is reduced by half or more, no Low-Fructose Fruit servings should be tracked. Due to their extremely low sugar content, lemons should not be reduced and do not need to be tracked.

STRAWBERRY MAGIC

1 Serving   Prep: 1 min   Blend: 2 min   Total: 3 min
4 Non-Starchy Vegetables   1 Nutrient-Dense Protein   1 Low-Fructose Fruit

- 1 Cup Strawberries (frozen or fresh)
- 2 Cups Arugula
- 4 Cups Spinach
- 1 Medium Lemon (peeled)
- 1/2 TSP Cinnamon
- 2 TBSP Garden in My Glass*
- 4 TBSP Clean Whey Protein**
- 1 TSP Hormone Healing Green Tea (optional)
- 2 TBSP Slimming Sugar Substitute (optional)***

DIRECTIONS

- Add all ingredients to a high-powered blender with 8 oz. cold water and a handful of ice.

- Blend for 2 minutes or until completely blended (i.e. no pieces of veggies or fruit are visible).

- Adjust the amount of water and ice for desired consistency and desired temperature.

TIP: Can't find some of these ingredients at your local grocery store? Have them delivered quickly and easily by visiting your SANE Superfoods Store at http://store.SANESolution.com.

NOTES

*You can add two additional serving of Non-Starchy Vegetables in place of the two tablespoons of Garden in My Glass. If you do not add more veggies and you do not add Garden in My Glass, track only two servings of Non-Starchy Vegetables per smoothie (instead of four servings).

**Only add protein if the smoothie is your entire meal. Vegetarians can use 6 TBSP of Clean Pea Protein (instead of Clean Whey Protein).

***To minimize sugar content, reduce fruit (other than lemon) and increase Slimming Sugar Substitute. If fruit is reduced by half or more, no Low-Fructose Fruit servings should be tracked. Due to their extremely low sugar content, lemons should not be reduced and do not need to be tracked.

STRAWBERRY ORANGE BLAST

1 Serving   Prep: 1 min   Blend: 2 min   Total: 3 min
4 Non-Starchy Vegetables   1 Nutrient-Dense Protein   1 Low-Fructose Fruit

- 1/2 Cup Strawberries (frozen or fresh)
- 1/2 Medium Orange (peeled)
- 6 Cups Spinach
- 1 Medium Lemon (peeled)
- 1/2 TSP Cinnamon
- 2 TBSP Garden in My Glass*
- 4 TBSP Clean Whey Protein**
- 1 TSP Hormone Healing Green Tea (optional)
- 2 TBSP Slimming Sugar Substitute (optional)***

DIRECTIONS

- Add all ingredients to a high-powered blender with 8 oz. cold water and a handful of ice.

- Blend for 2 minutes or until completely blended (i.e. no pieces of veggies or fruit are visible).

- Adjust the amount of water and ice for desired consistency and desired temperature.

TIP: Can't find some of these ingredients at your local grocery store? Have them delivered quickly and easily by visiting your SANE Superfoods Store at http://store.SANESolution.com.

NOTES

*You can add two additional serving of Non-Starchy Vegetables in place of the two tablespoons of Garden in My Glass. If you do not add more veggies and you do not add Garden in My Glass, track only two servings of Non-Starchy Vegetables per smoothie (instead of four servings).

**Only add protein if the smoothie is your entire meal. Vegetarians can use 6 TBSP of Clean Pea Protein (instead of Clean Whey Protein).

***To minimize sugar content, reduce fruit (other than lemon) and increase Slimming Sugar Substitute. If fruit is reduced by half or more, no Low-Fructose Fruit servings should be tracked. Due to their extremely low sugar content, lemons should not be reduced and do not need to be tracked.

STRAWBERRY ORANGE BLISS

1 Serving   Prep: 1 min   Blend: 2 min   Total: 3 min
4 Non-Starchy Vegetables   1 Nutrient-Dense Protein   1 Low-Fructose Fruit

- 1/2 Cup Strawberries (frozen or fresh)
- 1/2 Medium Orange (peeled)
- 2 Cups Arugula
- 4 Cups Romaine Lettuce
- 1 Medium Lemon (peeled)
- 1/2 TSP Cinnamon
- 2 TBSP Garden in My Glass*
- 4 TBSP Clean Whey Protein**
- 1 TSP Hormone Healing Green Tea (optional)
- 2 TBSP Slimming Sugar Substitute (optional)***

DIRECTIONS

- Add all ingredients to a high-powered blender with 8 oz. cold water and a handful of ice.

- Blend for 2 minutes or until completely blended (i.e. no pieces of veggies or fruit are visible).

- Adjust the amount of water and ice for desired consistency and desired temperature.

TIP: Can't find some of these ingredients at your local grocery store? Have them delivered quickly and easily by visiting your SANE Superfoods Store at http://store.SANESolution.com.

NOTES

*You can add two additional serving of Non-Starchy Vegetables in place of the two tablespoons of Garden in My Glass. If you do not add more veggies and you do not add Garden in My Glass, track only two servings of Non-Starchy Vegetables per smoothie (instead of four servings).

**Only add protein if the smoothie is your entire meal. Vegetarians can use 6 TBSP of Clean Pea Protein (instead of Clean Whey Protein).

***To minimize sugar content, reduce fruit (other than lemon) and increase Slimming Sugar Substitute. If fruit is reduced by half or more, no Low-Fructose Fruit servings should be tracked. Due to their extremely low sugar content, lemons should not be reduced and do not need to be tracked.

STRAWBERRY ORANGE ESCAPE

1 Serving   Prep: 1 min   Blend: 2 min   Total: 3 min
4 Non-Starchy Vegetables   1 Nutrient-Dense Protein   1 Low-Fructose Fruit

- 1/2 Cup Strawberries (frozen or fresh)
- 1/2 Medium Orange (peeled)
- 2 Cups Chard
- 4 Cups Spinach
- 1 Medium Lemon (peeled)
- 1/2 TSP Cinnamon
- 2 TBSP Garden in My Glass*
- 4 TBSP Clean Whey Protein**
- 1 TSP Hormone Healing Green Tea (optional)
- 2 TBSP Slimming Sugar Substitute (optional)***

DIRECTIONS

- Add all ingredients to a high-powered blender with 8 oz. cold water and a handful of ice.

- Blend for 2 minutes or until completely blended (i.e. no pieces of veggies or fruit are visible).

- Adjust the amount of water and ice for desired consistency and desired temperature.

TIP: Can't find some of these ingredients at your local grocery store? Have them delivered quickly and easily by visiting your SANE Superfoods Store at http://store.SANESolution.com.

NOTES

*You can add two additional serving of Non-Starchy Vegetables in place of the two tablespoons of Garden in My Glass. If you do not add more veggies and you do not add Garden in My Glass, track only two servings of Non-Starchy Vegetables per smoothie (instead of four servings).

**Only add protein if the smoothie is your entire meal. Vegetarians can use 6 TBSP of Clean Pea Protein (instead of Clean Whey Protein).

***To minimize sugar content, reduce fruit (other than lemon) and increase Slimming Sugar Substitute. If fruit is reduced by half or more, no Low-Fructose Fruit servings should be tracked. Due to their extremely low sugar content, lemons should not be reduced and do not need to be tracked.

STRAWBERRY ORANGE WHIRL

1 Serving   Prep: 1 min   Blend: 2 min   Total: 3 min
4 Non-Starchy Vegetables   1 Nutrient-Dense Protein   1 Low-Fructose Fruit

- 1/2 Cup Strawberries (frozen or fresh)
- 1/2 Medium Orange (peeled)
- 3 Cups Spinach
- 3 Cups Romaine Lettuce
- 1 Medium Lemon (peeled)
- 1/2 TSP Cinnamon
- 2 TBSP Garden in My Glass*
- 4 TBSP Clean Whey Protein**
- 1 TSP Hormone Healing Green Tea (optional)
- 2 TBSP Slimming Sugar Substitute (optional)***

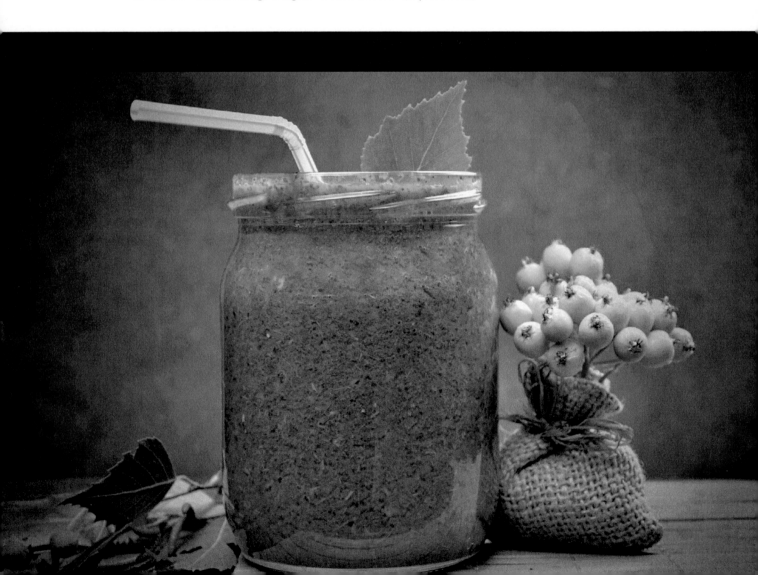

DIRECTIONS

- Add all ingredients to a high-powered blender with 8 oz. cold water and a handful of ice.

- Blend for 2 minutes or until completely blended (i.e. no pieces of veggies or fruit are visible).

- Adjust the amount of water and ice for desired consistency and desired temperature.

TIP: Can't find some of these ingredients at your local grocery store? Have them delivered quickly and easily by visiting your SANE Superfoods Store at http://store.SANESolution.com.

NOTES

*You can add two additional serving of Non-Starchy Vegetables in place of the two tablespoons of Garden in My Glass. If you do not add more veggies and you do not add Garden in My Glass, track only two servings of Non-Starchy Vegetables per smoothie (instead of four servings).

**Only add protein if the smoothie is your entire meal. Vegetarians can use 6 TBSP of Clean Pea Protein (instead of Clean Whey Protein).

***To minimize sugar content, reduce fruit (other than lemon) and increase Slimming Sugar Substitute. If fruit is reduced by half or more, no Low-Fructose Fruit servings should be tracked. Due to their extremely low sugar content, lemons should not be reduced and do not need to be tracked.

STRAWBERRY SUNRISE

1 Serving   Prep: 1 min   Blend: 2 min   Total: 3 min
4 Non-Starchy Vegetables   1 Nutrient-Dense Protein   1 Low-Fructose Fruit

- 1 Cup Strawberries (frozen or fresh)
- 6 Cups Romaine Lettuce
- 1 Medium Lemon (peeled)
- 1/2 TSP Cinnamon
- 2 TBSP Garden in My Glass*
- 4 TBSP Clean Whey Protein**
- 1 TSP Hormone Healing Green Tea (optional)
- 2 TBSP Slimming Sugar Substitute (optional)***

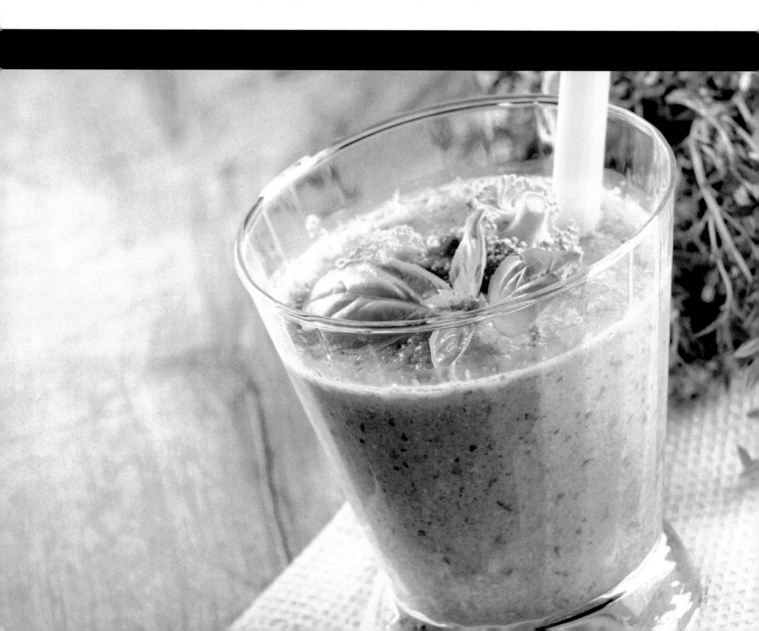

Directions

- Add all ingredients to a high-powered blender with 8 oz. cold water and a handful of ice.

- Blend for 2 minutes or until completely blended (i.e. no pieces of veggies or fruit are visible).

- Adjust the amount of water and ice for desired consistency and desired temperature.

TIP: Can't find some of these ingredients at your local grocery store? Have them delivered quickly and easily by visiting your SANE Superfoods Store at http://store.SANESolution.com.

Notes

*You can add two additional serving of Non-Starchy Vegetables in place of the two tablespoons of Garden in My Glass. If you do not add more veggies and you do not add Garden in My Glass, track only two servings of Non-Starchy Vegetables per smoothie (instead of four servings).

**Only add protein if the smoothie is your entire meal. Vegetarians can use 6 TBSP of Clean Pea Protein (instead of Clean Whey Protein).

***To minimize sugar content, reduce fruit (other than lemon) and increase Slimming Sugar Substitute. If fruit is reduced by half or more, no Low-Fructose Fruit servings should be tracked. Due to their extremely low sugar content, lemons should not be reduced and do not need to be tracked.

So Much To Look Forward To...

You will learn much more about this as we start your personal weight-loss plan together in your free half-day Masterclass (reserve your seat at SANESeminar.com), but here are a few key reminders as you're getting started on your SANE journey.

SANE eating is a lifelong, enjoyable, sustainable, simple, and delicious way of eating. **It is not a repackaging of the unsustainable calorie counting diets that failed you.**

I know you understand this already—otherwise you wouldn't be here—but please keep in mind that since SANE isn't a calorie counting diet, you will not suffer through the same calorie counting tools and resources that failed you in the past. For example, **memorizing endless food lists and following unrealistic minute-by-minute meal plans aren't just a pain—they cannot work in the real world**, and they cannot work long term.

Life is crazy. Things happen. And heck, people have different tastes in food, so while minute-by-minute "eat exactly this right now no matter what" endless lists might make for good reality TV, if they worked in the real world, you would have already met your goals. **To get a different result (long-term fat loss and robust health), you MUST take a different approach.** That's what you will find here.

If you approach your new SANE life calmly, gradually, and with the next 30 years in mind rather than the next 30 days, **you will learn the underlying principles that enable you to make the SANE choices easily—forever**.

Think of your new approach as the difference between memorizing the sum of every possible combination of numbers versus learning the underlying principles of how addition works. Once you understand addition, lists and memorization aren't necessary as you know what to do with any combination of numbers—forever.

The same thing applies with food. Once you understand the new science of SANE eating, **you will know exactly what to eat (and what to avoid) everywhere you go—forever—without any lists** or any memorization.

This new approach changes everything and will forever free you from all the confusing and conflicting weight-loss information you've been told. So please allow me to congratulate you on coming to the life-changing realization that **to get different results than you've gotten in the past, you must take a different approach than you used in the past!**

The great news is that when you combine a calm, gradual, long-term, and progress vs. perfection mindset with your scientifically proven SANE tools, program, and coaching, you are **guaranteed to burn belly fat, boost energy, and enjoy an unstoppable sense of self-confidence!**

Your new SANE lifestyle has helped over 100,000 people in over 37 countries burn fat and boost health *long-term.…*and it will do the same for you if you let it and trust it.

Thank you for taking the road less travelled…it will make all the difference!

SANEly and Gratefully,

Jonathan Bailor | SANE Founder, NYTimes Bestselling Author, and soon…your personal weight-loss coach

P.S. Over the years I have found that our most successful members, the ones who have lost 60, 70, even 100 pounds… and kept it off… are the ones who start their personal weight-loss plan on…

our FREE half-day Masterclass. It's your best opportunity to fall in love with the SANE lifestyle, learn exactly how to start making the simple changes that lead to dramatic body transformations, and get introduced to your new SANE family. Be sure to reserve your spot at http://SANESeminar.com.

Please Don't Lose Your Seat at the FREE Masterclass Seminar!

Reserve your spot now so we can start your perfect personalized weight-loss plan. Space is limited and fills-up quickly. Reserve your spot now so you don't miss out!

Yes! I want to reserve my spot now at SANESeminar.com

About the Author: Jonathan Bailor is a New York Times bestselling author and internationally recognized natural weight loss expert who specializes in using modern science and technology to simplify health. Bailor has collaborated with top scientists for more than 10 years to analyze and apply over 1,300 studies. His work has been endorsed by top doctors and scientists from Harvard Medical School, Johns' Hopkins, The Mayo Clinic, The Cleveland Clinic, and UCLA.

Bailor is the founder of SANESolution.com and serves as the CEO for the wellness technology company Yopti®. He authored the New York Times and USA Today bestselling book *The Calorie Myth*, hosts a popular syndicated health radio show *The SANE Show*, and blogs on *The Huffington Post*. Additionally, Bailor has registered over 25 patents, spoken at Fortune 100 companies and TED conferences for over a decade, and served as a Senior Program Manager at Microsoft where he helped create Nike+ Kinect Training and XBox Fitness.

Improve Your Weight Loss, Energy, Mood, and Digestion In Just 17 Second A Day!

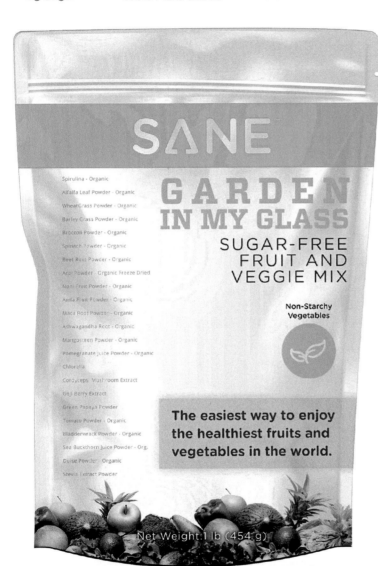

Introducing *Garden In My Glass*. The quickest, easiest, and most affordable way to get your family eating their fruits and veggies...and loving it!

When you order today you will also receive our wildly popular *'28 Days Of Green Smoothies'* recipe collection.

Plus, Get A Green Smoothie Recipe Book for FREE!

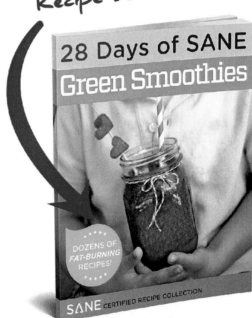

LEARN MORE AT: GardenInMyGlass.com

If You Are Ready To Get Off The Yo-Yo Diet Roller-coaster, Then It's Time To Start Your PERSONALIZED WEIGHT LOSS PLAN With Me!

Live Half-Day Seminar Tickets Cost ~~$397~~, But For A Limited Time, You Can Attend Online For FREE!

During Our Time Together You Will...

Free yourself from all the confusion and conflicting weight loss information! See the latest science showing you how to get off the yo-yo diet roller-coaster for good, while you overcome emotional eating and cravings.

Learn simple ways to jump-start your motivation today! I'll show you how to effortlessly stick with your new Personalized Weight Loss Plan for lasting results that turn heads and get attention.

Start creating your own personalized weight loss plan--with my help--that will show you exactly how many pounds you can lose per week and even give you an exact date when you will reach your goal weight...without ever counting calories, being hungry, or spending endless hours in the gym!

Discover the one "adjustment" you can make today to increase your energy and ignite your natural fat-burning metabolism so you jump out of bed every morning with confidence.

Crush cravings and end emotional eating with just a few small changes to the types of sweets and fats you are eating. Don't give up what you love, eat more...smarter! Bust the top myths and mistakes that hold you back from losing weight and keeping it off. (You will be relieved when we finally put these lies to rest).

Plus, just for attending you will receive the entire $297 Eat More Lose More Quick Start kit, with videos, cheat sheets, and food guide, for free so you can put this life-changing information to use immediately.

Getting Started Is Easy and Free:
There are many convenient times available

1. Type in this web address: SANESeminar.com
2. Click the button and select a convenient time
3. Enter your information to reserve your seat!

Made in the USA
San Bernardino, CA
20 March 2017